Whole-Rock Analyses of Core Samples from the 1988 Drilling of Kilauea Iki Lava Lake, Hawaii

By Rosalind Tuthill Helz and Joseph E. Taggart, Jr.

Open-File Report 2010–1093

U.S. Department of the Interior
U.S. Geological Survey

U.S. Department of the Interior
KEN SALAZAR, Secretary

U.S. Geological Survey
Marcia K. McNutt, Director

U.S. Geological Survey, Reston, Virginia 2010

For product and ordering information:
World Wide Web: http://www.usgs.gov/pubprod
Telephone: 1-888-ASK-USGS

For more information on the USGS—the Federal source for science about the Earth,
its natural and living resources, natural hazards, and the environment:
World Wide Web: http://www.usgs.gov
Telephone: 1-888-ASK-USGS

Suggested citation:
Helz, R.T., and Taggart, J.E., Jr., 2010, Whole-rock analyses of core samples from the 1988 drilling of Kilauea Iki lava lake, Hawaii: U.S. Geological Survey Open-File Report 2010–1093, 47 p.

Contents

Figures

Tables

Appendix Tables

Whole-Rock Analyses of Core Samples from the 1988 Drilling of Kilauea Iki Lava Lake, Hawaii

By Rosalind Tuthill Helz and Joseph E. Taggart, Jr.

Introduction

This report presents and evaluates 64 major-element analyses of previously unanalyzed Kilauea Iki drill core, plus three samples from the 1959 and 1960 eruptions of Kilauea, obtained by X-ray fluorescence (XRF) analysis during the period 1992 to 1995. All earlier major-element analyses of Kilauea Iki core, obtained by classical (gravimetric) analysis, were reported and evaluated in Helz and others (1994). In order to assess how well the newer data compare with this earlier suite of analyses, a subset of 24 samples, which had been analyzed by classical analysis, was reanalyzed using the XRF technique; those results are presented and evaluated in this report also. The XRF analyses have not been published previously. This report also provides an overview of how the chemical variations observed in these new data fit in with the chemical zonation patterns and petrologic processes inferred in earlier studies of Kilauea Iki.

Background and Previous Work

Kilauea Iki lava lake formed during the 1959 eruption of Kilauea Volcano, when lava ponded in the previously existing Kilauea Iki pit crater, located just east of the summit caldera (fig. 1). The eruption was closely observed and has been extensively documented (Richter and others, 1970; Eaton and others, 1987). Many samples of lava and pumice were collected during the eruption, and 23 samples of this material were analyzed and described by Murata and Richter (1966). Wright (1973) and Helz (1987a) have looked at the role of magma mixing during this eruption, using the bulk chemical data of Murata and Richter (1966) and Helz and others (1994), plus phase chemistry obtained using the electron microprobe.

Kilauea Iki lava lake remained accessible throughout the period of its cooling and crystallization (from 1959 to the mid-1990s) and so has been drilled repeatedly. The earliest core, recovered in 1960–1962, was described by Richter and Moore (1966), who presented 20 major-element analyses of the core, plus petrographic and modal data. Subsequent drilling was carried out in 1967, 1975, 1976, 1979, 1981, and 1988. The locations of the resulting drill holes are shown in plan view in figure 2 and in cross section in figure 3. Further details on the drilling, plus petrographic logs of the cores, are given in Helz and others (1984) for the 1967–1979 cores, in Helz and Wright (1983) for the 1981 cores, and in Helz (1993) for the 1988 cores.

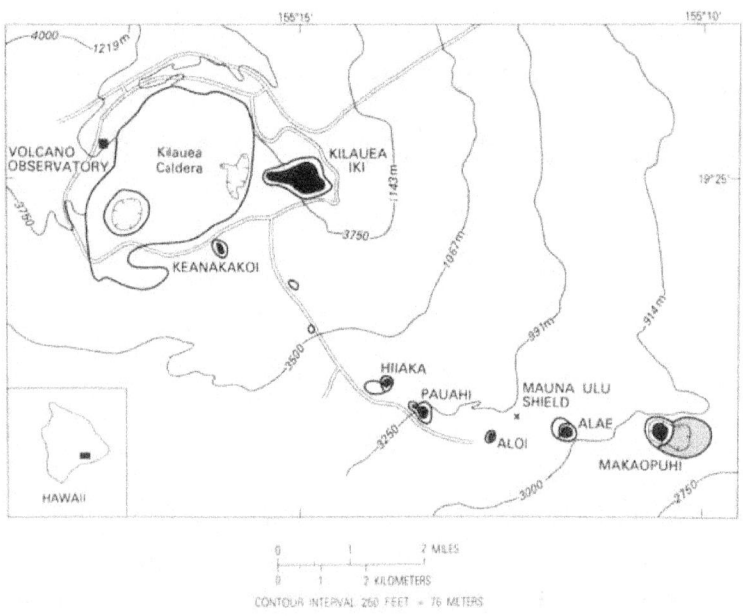

Figure 1. Index map of the summit area of Kilauea Volcano. All historic lava lakes are shown in black. The prehistoric Makaopuhi lava lake is shown in a stippled pattern. The historic lava lakes in Aloi, Alae, and Makaopuhi pit craters are now covered by lavas from the Mauna Ulu satellite shield, the summit of which is indicated by the "X."

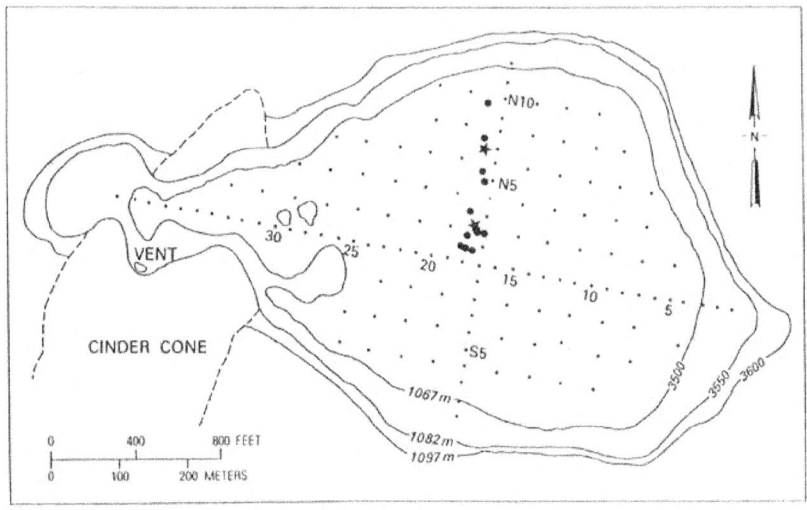

Figure 2. Plan view of the post-1959 surface of Kilauea Iki lava lake. The lake surface has a network of leveling stations, shown by the small dots. Larger dots indicate the locations of holes drilled from 1967 to 1981. The stars mark the locations of the two holes drilled in 1988.

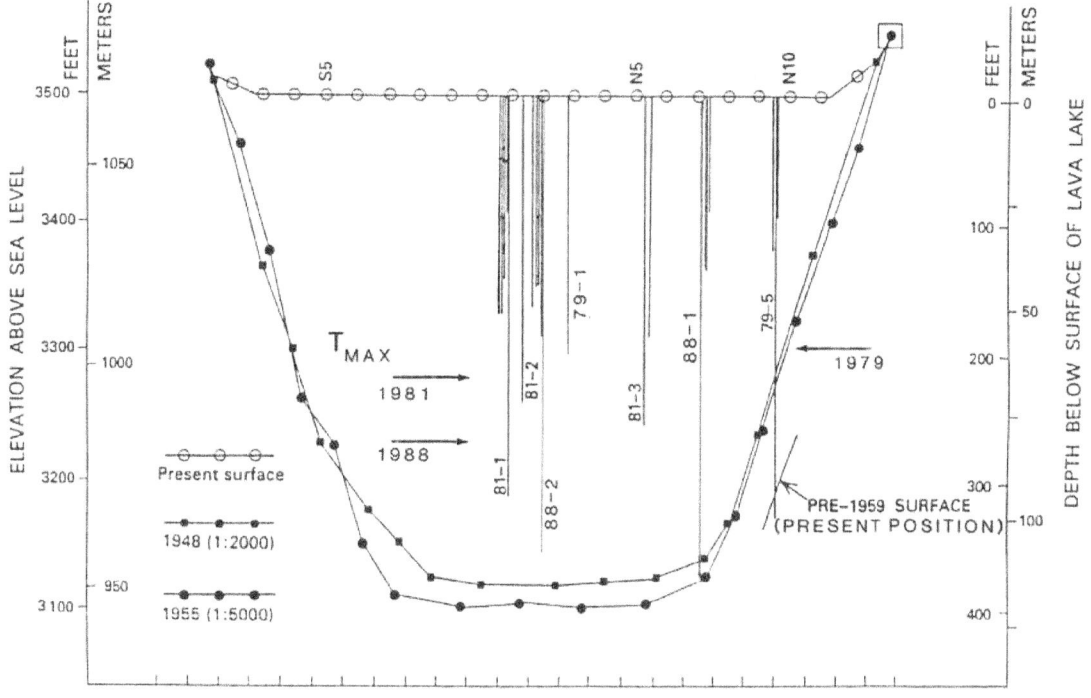

Figure 3. Cross section of Kilauea Iki lava lake taken along the north-south line of closely spaced leveling stations shown in figure 2. The present surface of the lava lake and two pre-eruption profiles are shown. The two pre-eruption profiles are taken from two different topographic maps: one (at 1:2000) is based on air photos taken in 1948; the other (at 1:5000) is based on air photos taken in 1955, as indicated. Both maps were prepared by R. Jordan, USGS, Flagstaff, AZ. The present position of the lake bottom has been intersected only at the location of drill hole KI79-5 and lies 20–23 m deeper here and across the flat central floor than the pre-eruptive topography would suggest (see discussion in Helz, 1993). Vertical exaggeration is 4:1.

The drill holes are shown as vertical lines projected onto this cross section. Several of the drilling locations have been reoccupied more than once; spacing between closely spaced holes is not to scale in this figure. Only the deepest hole in each cluster has been labeled, for clarity. The arrows mark the position of the thermal maximum (T_{MAX}) in 1979, 1981, and 1988 as determined by analyzing glass in quenched, partially molten drill core using the glass geothermometer of Helz and Thornber (1987).

These cores have been studied extensively, using petrography and microprobe analysis of individual phases, as well as chemical analysis of bulk samples. The results of studies based on the 1967–1981 cores were reported in Helz (1980; 1987a, b), Helz and Thornber (1987), Helz and others (1989), Helz and others (1994), and Barth and others (1994). More recently, Kilauea Iki samples have been used in a range of isotopic and trace element studies, including Teng and others (2007, 2008) and Pitcher and others (2009). The first paper to make use of the analytical results for the 1988 core is Helz (2009).

Sampling Procedures – 1988 Core

The U.S. Geological Survey (USGS) drilled two holes in 1988, as shown in figures 2 and 3. Because Kilauea Iki lava lake had reached an advanced state of crystallization by that time, it was possible to drill completely through the partially molten lens in the middle of the lake and into the lower crust (Helz, 1993), although neither hole passed through the entire lake. These cores extend to greater depths than any obtained earlier and provide the first significant sampling of the lower crust (as defined by the position of the maximum temperature encountered, see fig. 3) of the lava lake.

The 1988 drill core was sampled for analysis, generally at intervals of 10 feet (ft; 3.0 meters (m)), to supplement analytical coverage obtained and reported by Helz and others (1994). Accordingly, core KI88-1, from 30 ft (8.8 m) south of a location previously drilled in 1967 and 1975 (cores KI67-1 and KI75-2), was extensively sampled from 40 ft down to the bottom of the hole at 376 ft (12.2 to 114.6 m), and 38 samples were analyzed.

KI88-2 (see fig. 3 for location) was drilled at the hottest known part of the lake in order to sample the widest possible partially molten interval available in 1988. This hole is near a cluster of earlier holes that was shown by glass geothermometry (Helz and Thornber, 1987) to be hotter than any other section sampled. Earlier cores from this cluster were examined petrographically and by microprobe analysis but were not submitted for whole-rock chemical analysis. Core from KI88-2 was sampled to supplement analytical data available from the main cluster (KI67-3, KI75-1, KI79-3, KI81-1) 104 ft (31.7 m) to the south and from the single drill hole KI79-1, 93 ft (28.3 m) to the north. Sampling of KI88-2 began at about 150 ft (45.7 m) and continued to the bottom of the hole at 355 ft (108.2 m) with a total of 24 samples analyzed.

Analytical samples were cut from the core with a diamond saw blade, using water as the coolant. All subsequent sample preparation (grinding, splitting) was performed in the analytical laboratories of the USGS in Reston, VA, as described in Taylor and Theodorakos (2002). The material selected was in most cases intended to be representative of the 10-ft interval from which it came. In places where the core was visibly heterogeneous, containing internal differentiates [segregation veins, vorbs (vertical, olivine-rich bodies), and melt chimneys or speckled-rock plumes (see discussion in Helz, 1993)], care was taken that the analytical sample be uniform in character, either completely normal or consisting only of the variant rock type.

Analytical Methods

The new analyses presented here were obtained by X-ray fluorescence (XRF) analysis in the USGS analytical laboratory in Denver, CO, between 1992 and 1995, using the method described in Taggart and others (1987) and Taggart and Siems (2002). The analyses presented here for jobs CJ12 and CJ13 include the complete "X-ray support package" consisting of determinations for FeO, CO_2 and $H_2O\pm$, obtained following the methods outlined in Jackson and others (1987). The results for job WC69 include FeO but not determinations of CO_2 and $H_2O\pm$.

In addition to the above, the analyses include determinations for Cl, F, and Cr. Cl was analyzed using the selective ion electrode (SIE) method outlined in Jackson and others (1987), while F was analyzed using the SIE method of Kirschenbaum (1988). The Cr analyses in jobs CJ12 and CJ13 were obtained by inductively coupled plasma-atomic emission spectrometry (ICP-AES) following the method described in Lichte and others (1987), while Cr in job WC69 was obtained by XRF. Analytical results for these three elements were obtained in laboratories in Reston, VA, and Menlo Park, CA.

Many analytical chemists of the USGS contributed to the three jobs that make up this dataset. The major-element XRF data were produced by J.S. Mee and D.F. Siems. The "X-ray support package" work plus the Cl and F determinations were performed by M.G. Kavulak, C.J. Skeen, J.R. Gillison, H. Smith, T.R. Peacock, and J.H. Bullock. The Cr analyses were done by M.W. Doughten and J. Kent.

As mentioned above, all earlier whole-rock analyses for core samples from Kilauea Iki or pumices from the 1959 eruption were analyzed by classical, gravimetric techniques (Peck, 1964; Kirschenbaum, 1983). When it became necessary to switch to the XRF method for the 1988 core, there was some concern that the new data might not be consistent with the 176 analyses in the earlier dataset. An attempt to cross-check the results of the newer technique against the old, to see if there were any offsets or biases between the two, was made in early 1992. At that time a selection of 24 previously analyzed powders, from many earlier jobs and including the work of all of the chemists involved in the classical analyses, was submitted to J.E. Taggart, Jr., for redetermination of the major elements by XRF. These samples were not reanalyzed for FeO, CO_2, $H_2O\forall$, Cl, F, and Cr, as the sole purpose of the resubmission was to cross-calibrate the XRF and gravimetric major element data.

Description of the Analytical Tables

The analytical tables are presented at the end of this report. Tables A1 and A2 contain all analyses from cores KI88-1 and KI88-2, respectively. Table A3 contains analyses of two fill-in samples from drill core KI79-1, intended to supplement earlier sampling, plus a few eruption samples. Of these, Iki-3 from the 1959 eruption has never been analyzed before, while Iki-14 was represented in Murata and Richter (1966) by a "rapid-rock" analysis. The last sample included is KP-16, which erupted on January 29, 1960, and was analyzed to fill in a gap in the time series for the 1960 Puna eruption at Kilauea. The results of cross-checking the XRF major-element analyses with earlier classical analyses are shown in tables A4a–g, which include both analyses side by side, to facilitate comparison.

5

In all tables, core samples are identified by a field number of the form "KI88-1-41.4". This example designates a sample from core KI88-1, from a depth of 41.4 ft (12.52 m) below the surface of the lava lake. The "lab number" is an individual number assigned to the sample for purposes of sample control within the USGS analytical laboratory system. The job number shows which batches of samples were analyzed as a group. The three analytical jobs presented here are CJ12, CJ13, and WC69. Other job numbers indicate older analyses for various samples that are included in these tables for purposes of comparison with the new data.

The major-element data in tables A1–A3 are reported to three significant figures, and the results on additional minor elements are reported to two decimal places, as given in the analytical reports. A dash in the table indicates that the particular element was not determined for that sample. Where an element was analyzed for but not detected, the amount is indicated to be less than some limit (typically <0.01). In table A4, the classical analyses are reported as they were in Helz and others (1994), and the data for the 24 XRF rechecks are reported to the same number of decimal places, as given in that report.

XRF analysis cannot determine the different oxidation states of iron and customarily reports all iron as Fe_2O_3, regardless of the actual oxidation state of iron in the samples. The "support package" includes an independent determination of FeO in the samples, which permits calculation of the actual Fe_2O_3 content of the samples and allows calculation of a summation for the analysis. This is important as the analytical summation is a fairly basic indicator of the quality of an analysis (Taggart and Siems, 2002). Accordingly, in tables A1–A3, the results of the XRF majors and support package have been merged. The results for Cl, F, and Cr have also been added, with Cr recalculated as Cr_2O_3. All concentrations shown in plain type in tables A1–A3 have been included in the summations presented. Because no CO_2 or H_2O contents were obtained for analytical job WC69, these components have not been included in any of the summations, in order to make the results comparable for all three jobs.

In table A4, by contrast, all iron in the classical analyses has been recalculated to Fe_2O_3, in order to facilitate direct comparison with the XRF results. In this table, summations have been omitted because the minor elements were not redetermined and because total iron as Fe_2O_3 produces summations that are systematically too high, as most iron in these iron-rich samples is ferrous.

Additional information on each sample is provided below the analyses. Most samples of 1988 core were selected to be typical of the 10-ft interval in which they are found. Specific designations indicate whether (1) the sample is interpreted to be foundered crust (see discussion in Helz, 1993) or adjacent to foundered crust, (2) the sample is the one closest to the observed thermal maximum in the core, (3) the sample lies immediately above or below an overnight stop in the drilling, or (4) the sample is a sample of cross-cutting diapirs ("vorb" or speckled-rock plume). In addition, most samples have been assigned a zone number, based on the chemical zonation developed in Helz and others (1989) and discussed later in this report. In table A4, special sample designations are those used in Helz and others (1994) and are explained in that reference.

The tables also note whether the sample analyzed contains glass (quenched melt) or not. Finally the core has been put into one of three categories, depending on its pre-quenching temperature. "High" samples are those quenched from temperatures above the solidus, which lies at 970–980 degrees Celsius (^{o}C); these contain glass interpreted as having been a stable melt phase prior to quenching. "Medium" samples are those quenched from temperatures below the solidus but above the boiling point of water (approximately 110 °C for the geothermal system in the lake, as the water contains some dissolved salts). "Low" temperature samples are those that were quenched from 110 °C and, hence, had been in contact with liquid water prior to drilling. This information is included because it bears on the freshness of the material analyzed, though all Kilauea Iki core is pristine by normal geologic standards.

Quality of the Analyses

Cross-Check with Classical Analyses

As noted above, 24 samples previously analyzed by classical techniques were resubmitted for XRF majors in early 1992, in order to cross-calibrate the two techniques; the data are reported in table A4a–g. The samples chosen covered all older analytical jobs and all analysts, and most appeared to be excellent analyses (Helz and others, 1994). However, three samples were included because there seemed to be one or more problems with the original analyses. Based on the XRF major-element results for those three samples, which confirmed the problems suspected, an additional five samples were resubmitted as part of job CJ13, in order to check their analyses as well. All samples rechecked "for cause" are listed in table 1, and the results are included in table A4a–g.

Table 1. Kilauea Iki samples for which the classical analysis was rechecked by XRF for cause, with suspect elements indicated.

Sample	First job	New job	Element checked
KI67-2-0.5	BR98	cross-check	Al high, Fe low
KI67-2-17.0	BD25	CJ13	Ti low
KI67-2-40.4	BD25	cross-check	Ti low
KI67-2-59.8	BD25	CJ13	Ti, Fe for consistency with previous three samples
KI79-1-141.0	BK52	cross-check	Si high, sum high
KI79-1-160	BK52	CJ13	Si high, sum high
KI79-1-170	BK52	CJ13	Si high, sum high
KI79-5-180.9	BD25	CJ13	Ti low

Table 2 compares the limits of error for each oxide in the classical analyses (Kirschenbaum, 1983; Flanagan and Kirschenbaum, 1984) and the reproducibility of XRF results for BHVO-1 (Thornber and others, 2002) with the average difference between the XRF and classical analyses in the cross-check set. The complete range of deviation is also given for each oxide (excluding the oxides in the few samples rechecked "for cause," as noted in table 1). The results show that in general the average difference between the XRF and classical analyses is similar in size to the limit of error of the classical analysis. Note, however, that the range is not always symmetrical around the classical values.

Table 2. Comparison of the limits of error for classical analysis, average difference and range observed between XRF and classical analyses in cross-check batch, with reproducibility of XRF major-element analyses for rock standard BHVO-1. All quantities in weight percent.

Component oxide	Limits of error (Kirschenbaum, 1983)	Average deviation	Range (XRF– classical)	BHVO-1 (Thornber and others, 2002)
SiO_2	±0.10	+0.08	–0.47 to +0.42	±0.14
TiO_2	±0.03	+0.03	–0.04 to +0.07	±0.011
Al_2O_3	±0.15	–0.17	–0.45 to +0.14	±0.05
Fe_2O_3	±0.08	+0.15	–0.04 to +0.29	±0.03
MgO	±0.05	+0.10	–0.13 to +0.32	±0.06
CaO	±0.05	–0.09	–0.24 to +0.02	±0.03
Na_2O	±0.03	–0.04	–0.14 to +0.07	±0.06
K_2O	±0.03	+0.006	–0.03 to +0.08	±0.004
P_2O_5	±0.01	+0.02	–0.04 to +0.05	±0.011

The results of these cross-checks are shown graphically in figures 4a–j, one for each of the 10 elements determined by XRF. The values from the classical analyses are on the abscissa and the new XRF values on the ordinate; the diagonal (1:1) line shows where the results would be exactly equal. Two subsets are distinguished: the 21 "good" analyses are designated as "standards" and the 8 rechecks are identified separately. Comparison of the size of the symbols in figure 4 with the limits of error and average differences in table 2 shows that the symbols used in these figures are larger than the uncertainties.

Figure 4a shows that the agreement between the two methods for MgO is very good, without any systematic offset from the 1:1 line. This is important, as MgO varies in these samples by an order of magnitude and is used as the abscissa in most chemical variation diagrams for Hawaiian basalts (see for example Wright, 1971, or Wright and Fiske, 1971, in addition to the papers on Kilauea Iki cited earlier). By contrast, the results for CaO (fig. 4b) show that the XRF determinations run slightly lower (by 0.09 on average, table 2) than the classical CaO values.

8

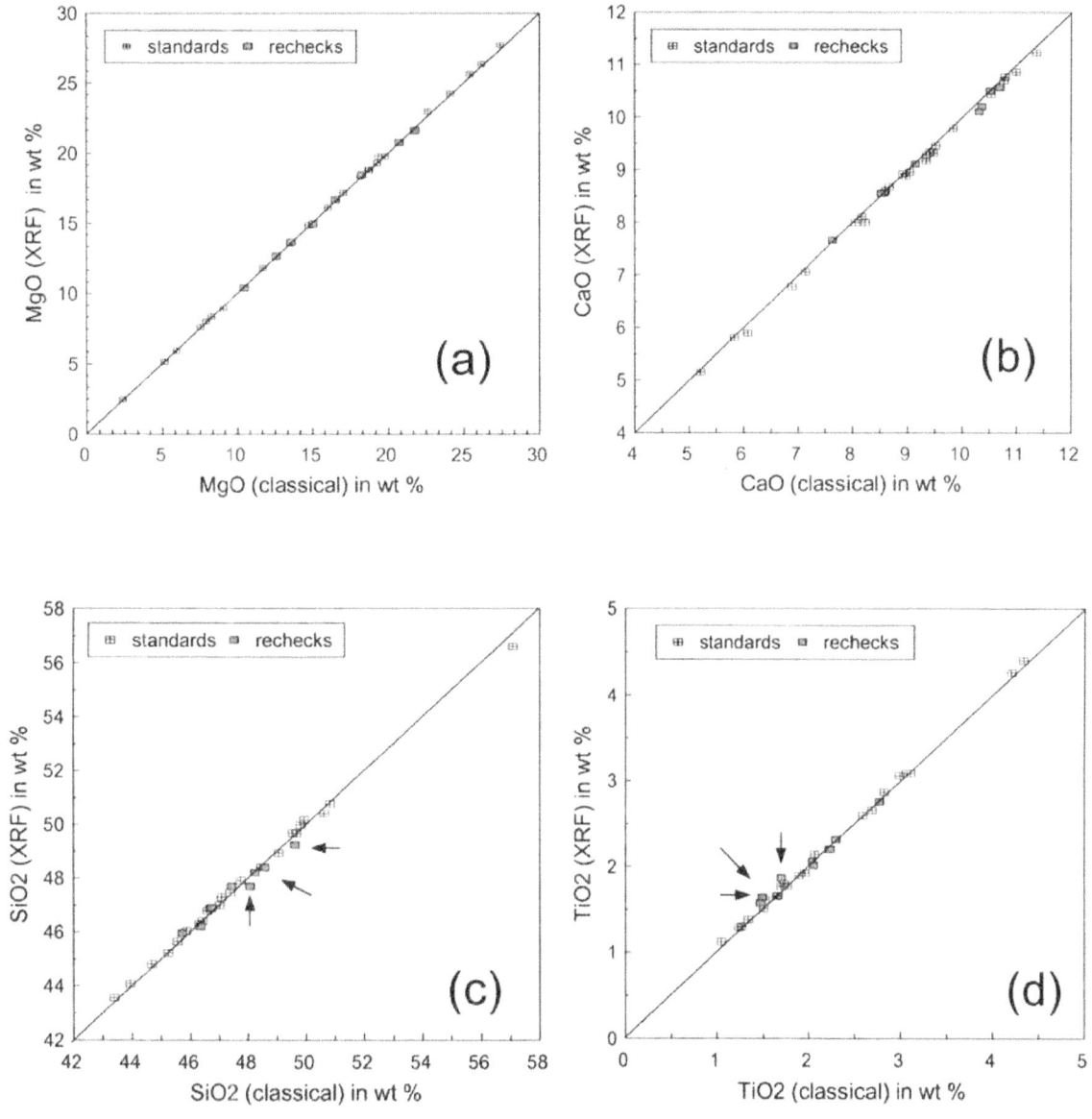

Figure 4. (a–j) Whole-rock classical values of major oxides plotted against XRF values for each oxide, for data in table A4. Samples rechecked for cause are flagged by arrows in the plot for the element at issue. All quantities are in weight percent.

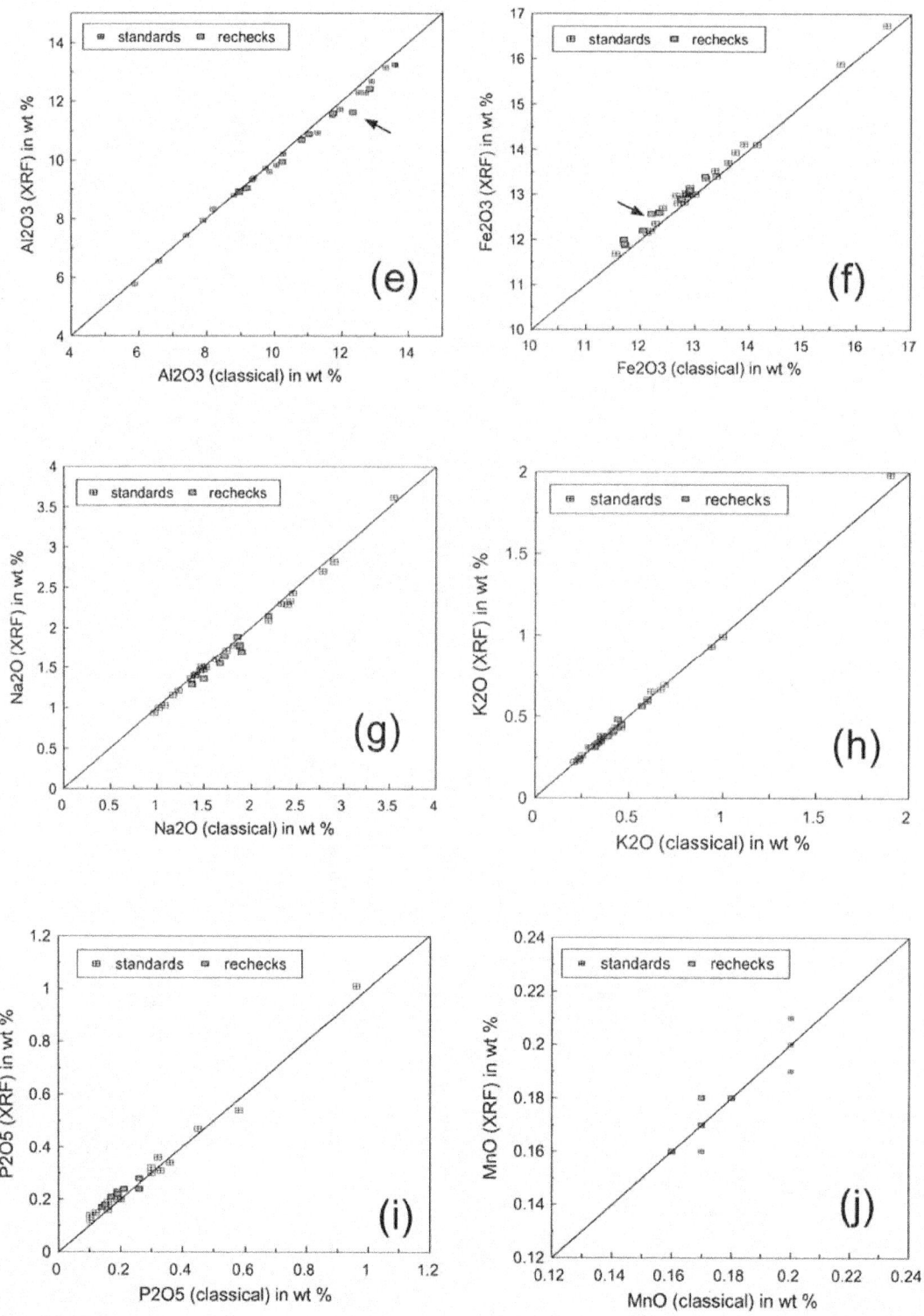

The agreement between the two methods for SiO_2 is generally quite good. Three samples where the classical value was suspected of being high (based in part on a high summation) do indeed lie below the 1:1 line in figure 4c. The only other analysis that falls on the low side is that for KI81-2-88.6, an extreme differentiate with $MgO = 2.4$ percent, with a bulk composition quite different from the rest of the samples from Kilauea Iki. The results for TiO_2 (fig. 4d) are similar to those for SiO_2: most samples fall very near the 1:1 line, and the three samples suspected of having low classical TiO_2 values fall distinctly above the 1:1 line, suggesting that the classical results were indeed somewhat low for those three samples.

Figures 4e (Al_2O_3) and 4f (Fe_2O_3) are paired because in the classical separation process, the "R_2O_3" group is precipitated together, with Fe_2O_3 and Cr_2O_3 determined separately and subtracted, and Al_2O_3 determined by difference (Peck, 1964; Kirschenbaum, 1983). Thus, an error in the Fe_2O_3 determination will generate the opposite error in Al_2O_3. For one sample (KI67-2-0.5), the cross-check results suggest that this did indeed happen, with the original Fe_2O_3 determination being too low. That sample aside, the Al_2O_3 values for the two methods agree very well below about 10 percent Al_2O_3, but veer below the 1:1 line at higher Al_2O_3 contents. The average difference is not large, but it is not random. Al_2O_3 in the classical analyses has been corrected for Cr_2O_3 (Helz and others, 1994), so its variation is not contributing to the pattern seen in figure 4e.

Fe_2O_3 (fig. 4f) does not show such a pattern but runs high in all the XRF analyses relative to the classical determinations by an amount that is twice the expected limit of error in the classical analyses (table 2). Given that the patterns of deviation for these two oxides are distinct, the offsets cannot be explained as reciprocal "R_2O_3" errors in the classical analyses.

Corresponding values for Na_2O (fig. 4g) and K_2O (fig. 4h) generally lie near the 1:1 correspondence line, with the standards and rechecks being similarly distributed. The XRF determination of K_2O in the extreme sample (KI81-2-88.6), which is 0.1 percent higher than the earlier analysis, lies farthest from the 1:1 line in figure 4h.

XRF values for P_2O_5 (fig. 4i) run higher than those obtained by classical methods, although the differences are small. MnO data are shown in figure 4j; because many analyses have the same limited range of values for MnO (0.16 to 0.20) by both methods, many samples plot on top of each other, giving the false impression that only eight samples exist. The two methods have produced comparable results for MnO.

In summary, for 6 (of 10) elements analyzed (MgO, SiO_2, TiO_2, Na_2O, K_2O, and MnO) the two types of analyses are closely comparable. CaO runs slightly low in the XRF analyses, while Fe_2O_3 and P_2O_5 run somewhat high. Al_2O_3 shows a variable trend distinct from the offset in Fe_2O_3 determinations. However, it appears from the cross-check data that XRF major and gravimetric analyses are close enough to form a coherent dataset for Kilauea Iki.

Coherence of the New Analyses: Summations

Moving now to evaluate the new XRF data in tables A1–A3, there are several ways to assess the overall coherence of the new analyses. The first and simplest is to look at the summations for the analyses, to see how they fall relative to the ideal summation of 100 percent, as discussed in Taggart and Siems (2002). Figure 5 shows the range of summations for the analyses in tables A1–A3. Because $H_2O\pm$ was not determined for job

WC69, those concentrations have been omitted from the summations for all analyses, both in the tables and in figure 5.

The two histograms in figure 5 are very different from that for the 176 classical (gravimetric) analyses (Helz and others, 1994), reproduced here in figure 6. First, the histograms for the XRF analyses do not have the symmetrical bell shape seen in the collection of classical analyses. Second, neither histogram is distributed around 100 percent: the summations mostly lie either above or below that value. Third, the batches are inconsistent, with the analyses in the first two batches (CJ12, CJ13) running systematically high in one or more components. It is suspected that this was caused by an inhomogeneity in the lithium tetraborate sample fusion discs. The portions of the flux containing higher concentrations of sample would have a greater density and would have settled to the bottom of the mold, causing the analytical surface of the disc to be more concentrated in all elements of the sample.

The off-center distributions in figure 5 may reflect the fact that the various analysts who contributed to the new analyses could not know the FeO and Fe_2O_3 concentrations in the sample and so did not have the information needed to see a complete total. For the classical gravimetric analyses, however, the analysts were mindful of the summations as they moved through the analytical procedure. Also, for the "R_2O_3" subset, the final component (Al_2O_3) was determined by difference (Kirschenbaum, 1983).

It is evident from the offset patterns and larger ranges of summations in figure 5 compared with figure 6 that the new analyses, though acceptably precise when compared oxide by oxide with the gravimetric analyses (as was done in the preceding section), may not be as accurate as the classical analyses.

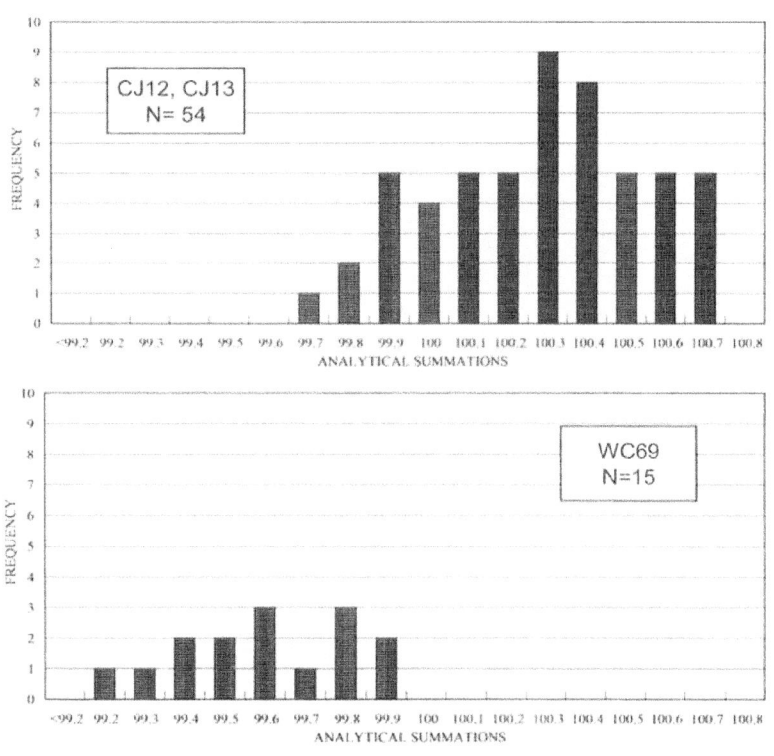

Figure 5. Frequency distribution of summations for XRF analyses of drill core from Kilauea Iki from tables A1–A3. $H_2O\pm$ has been omitted from all summations, as noted in the text.

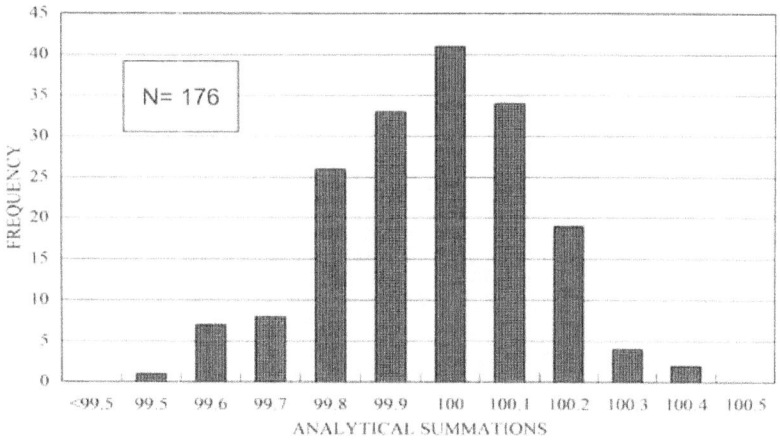

Figure 6. Frequency distribution of summations for classical (gravimetric) analyses of drill core from Kilauea Iki lava lake (Helz and others, 1994).

13

Figure 7 shows the summations from tables A1–A3 plotted against whole-rock MgO content, with the three analytical batches identified separately. The positive correlations between summation and MgO content suggest that there is some bias toward high MgO in the most MgO-rich samples. However, the range in MgO contents for jobs CJ12 + CJ13 versus WC69 is the same. Given that the range is similar and that the summations run about 0.5 percent higher across the entire range, it seems that MgO is not the only component that runs high, thus supporting the inhomogeneous fusion disc suggestion. At present it is not clear what has produced the 0.5 percent offset in summations, but it seems unlikely that this can be attributed to any one component in the analyses. Whatever the problem, it was not experienced by the analyst who ran job WC69.

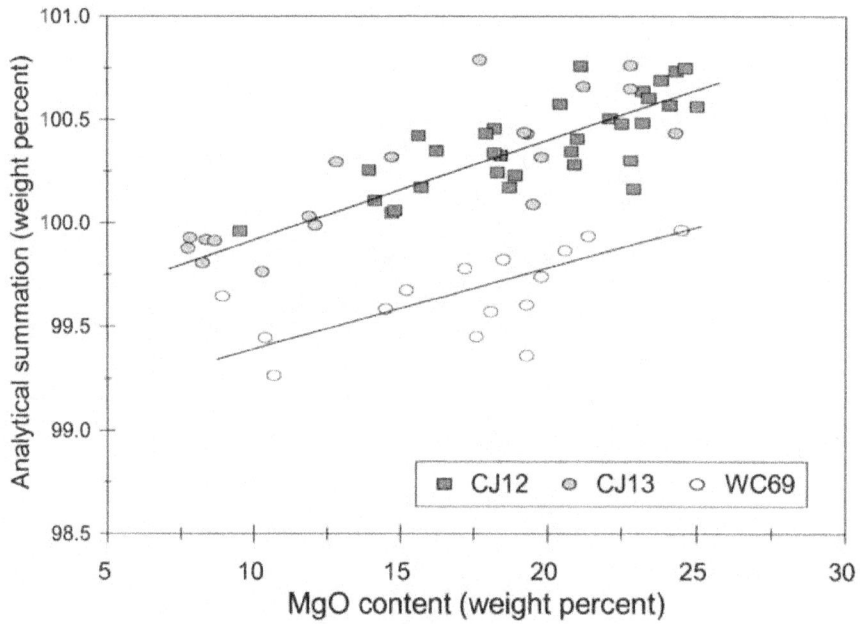

Figure 7. Analytical summations plotted against bulk MgO content for Kilauea Iki data in tables A1–A3.

Coherence of the New Analyses: Element Ratios

Another standard way of evaluating the coherence of a set of basalt analyses from Kilauea is to examine ratios that should be constant or nearly constant during high-temperature fractionation, as was discussed in Wright (1971). Useful ratios include P_2O_5/K_2O and P_2O_5/TiO_2, as the elements P, K, and Ti are largely absent from the early crystallizing minerals olivine $\pm$ chromite + augite + plagioclase. Figure 8 shows how these ratios vary for the XRF data presented in tables A1–A3. Note that the correlations are consistent across all three analytical jobs, further supporting the suggestion of the increased, but proportional, concentration of sample on the analytical surface of the fusion discs.

The results in figure 8, when compared with those in figures 5 and 6 of Helz and others (1994), show that the XRF and gravimetric analyses are similar. In both sets of analyses, the data fall on a line with a 1:10 slope for P_2O_5/TiO_2 and a 1:2 slope for P_2O_5/K_2O. These plots confirm that (1) fractionation of TiO_2 by crystallization of augite and of K_2O by crystallization of plagioclase have not affected the bulk compositions of these samples and (2) the XRF results are consistent with the earlier gravimetric analyses for these elements.

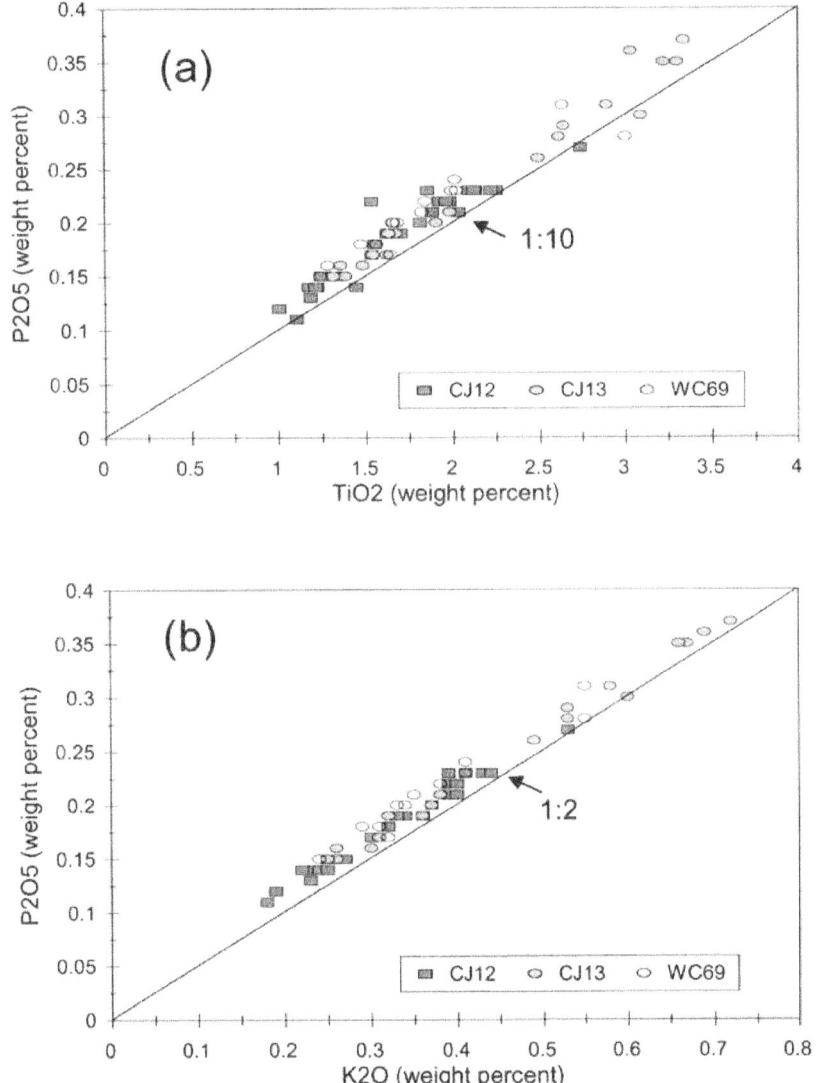

Figure 8. (a) Whole-rock P_2O_5 plotted against TiO_2 for analyses in tables A1–A3. (b) Whole-rock P_2O_5 plotted against K_2O for analyses in tables A1–A3.

15

Chemical Variations in Kilauea Iki Samples

The range and character of the chemical variations in drill core from Kilauea Iki lava lake can be displayed most effectively on a series of magnesia variation diagrams for several reasons, as discussed in Helz and others (1994). The most basic consideration is that MgO shows the largest range of concentrations of any major oxide, varying by an order of magnitude (from 2.4 to 27.4 percent by weight) for samples from Kilauea Iki. The range observed for analyses in this report is narrower (7.74 to 25.0 percent by weight), as no internal differentiates such as segregation veins were selected for analysis from the 1988 drill core. The range found here lies within the range where MgO content reflects variation in the amount of phenocrystic olivine in the rocks, as discussed in Helz (1987a) and Helz and others (1989).

Accordingly, figure 9 shows the variation of 10 major- and minor-element oxides, plus F and Cl, for MgO = 7.7 to 25.0 percent, for the analyses in tables A1–A3. In addition, the limits of composition of the 1959 eruption samples (as given in Wright, 1973) are shown for the eight major oxides. These limits outline the range of bulk compositions that would exist in the lake if variation in the amount of inherited olivine phenocrysts ($Fo_{86.5-87.0}$; as discussed in Murata and Richter, 1966; Wright, 1973; Helz, 1987b; Helz and others, 1989) were the only process affecting the samples.

In figure 9a (SiO_2 versus MgO) almost all samples fall within the range of the 1959 eruption samples. That is, they lie on a well-defined "olivine control line" (Wright, 1971) that reflects the composition of the original, inherited olivine phenocrysts. This was also true for all of the classical analyses with MgO > 7.0 percent. [The sole exception in either dataset is sample KI88-1-41.4, which runs low in SiO_2 (and high in total iron), for reasons that are not clear. This sample, in hand specimen and thin section, looks no different from adjacent core.] Thus olivine redistribution in the lake occurred prior to any significant reequilibration of olivine to more iron-rich compositions. This in turn means that olivine redistribution was an early process and occurred at temperatures close to original eruption temperatures (Helz, 2009). The variation of Cr_2O_3 with MgO (fig. 9c) is also controlled by this early process, because almost all Cr_2O_3 is present in chromite, found mostly as inclusions in the olivine phenocrysts, which then move with the olivine.

Concentrations of the other major oxides, including Al_2O_3, CaO, FeO, and TiO_2, have all been affected by one or more additional differentiation processes occurring in Kilauea Iki. The most important of these is diapiric melt transfer, in which a minimum-density melt, which is produced near the temperature where plagioclase begins to crystallize, migrates from the base of the partially molten core of the lake to the base of the upper crystallization front. This process was first proposed and documented in Helz and others (1989). Its effect on the concentration of the platinum group elements and Re in Kilauea Iki was discussed in Pitcher and others (2009), and the interactions between this process and other styles of differentiation that occur in the lava lake are explored in Helz (2009).

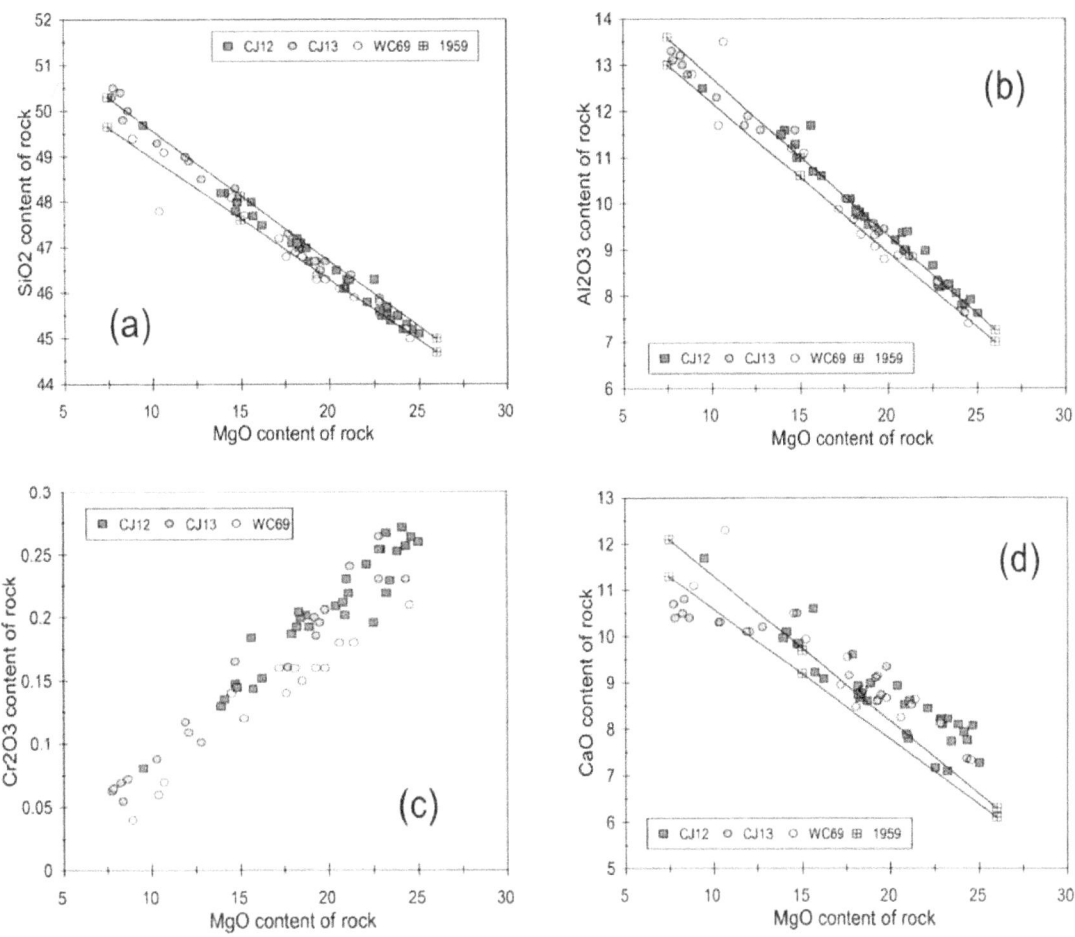

Figure 9 (a-l). Oxide–oxide plots showing the compositional variation of samples described in this report as a function of their MgO contents. The first three symbols correspond to the three analytical batches in tables A1–A3. The boxes labeled "1959" outline the compositional range of the 1959 eruption samples, as given in Wright (1973). The 1959 field is not defined for the minor components Cr_2O_3, MnO, F, and Cl. All quantities are in weight percent.

17

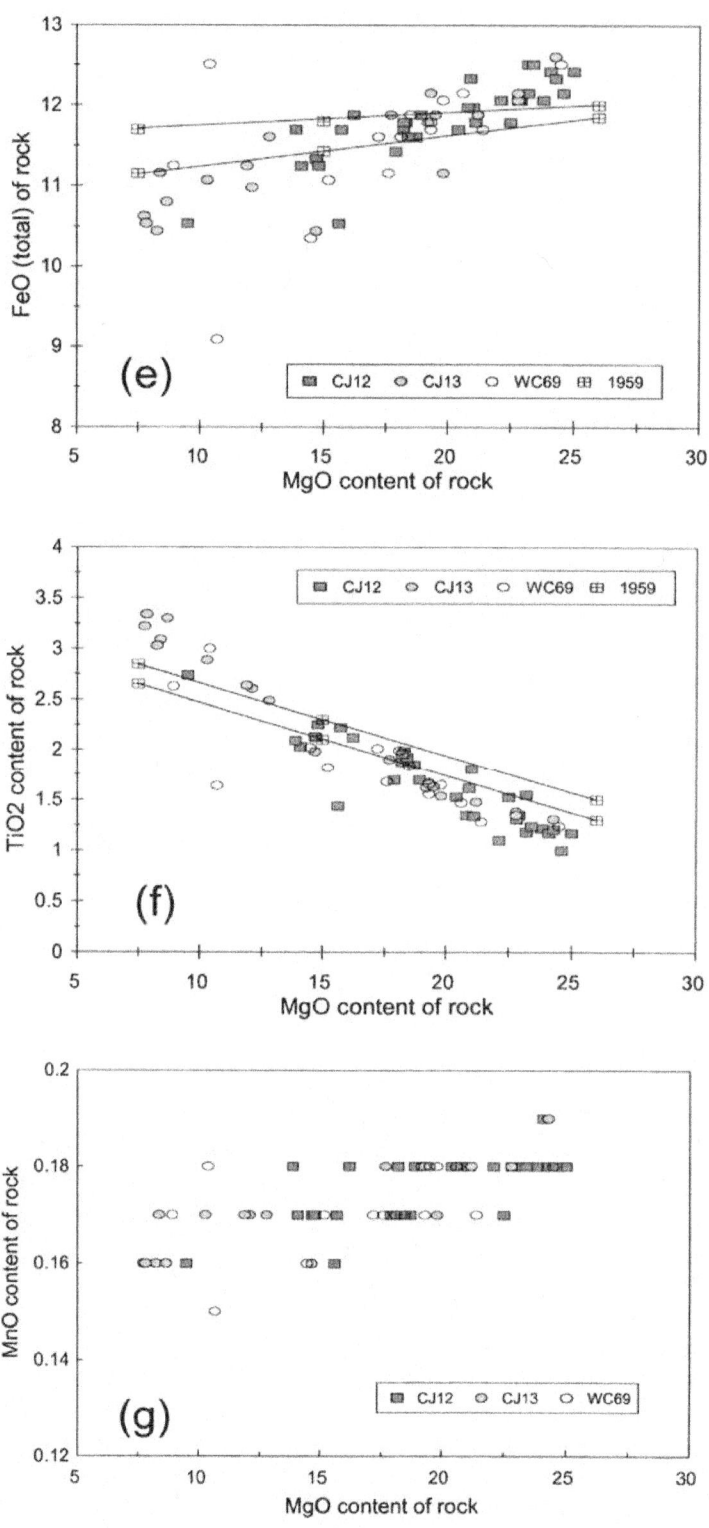

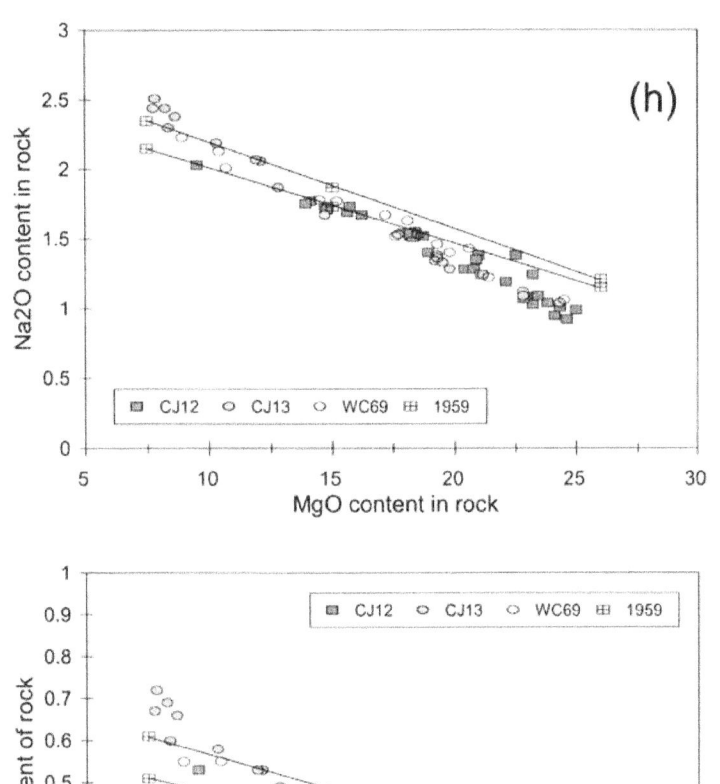

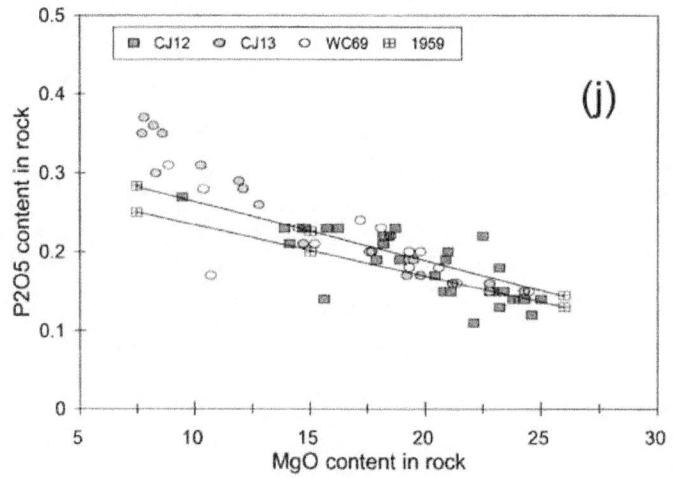

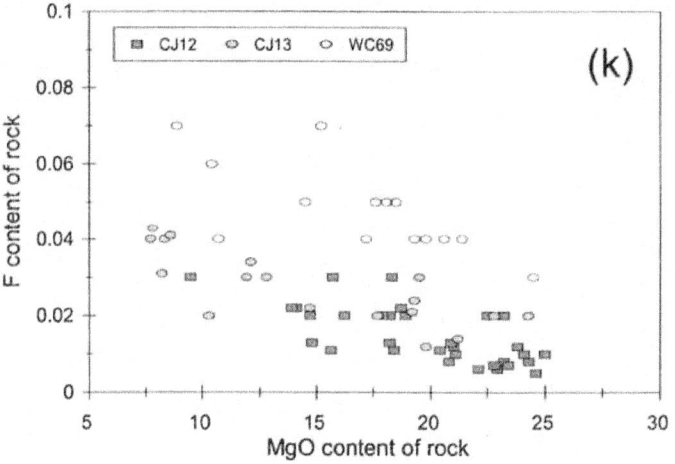

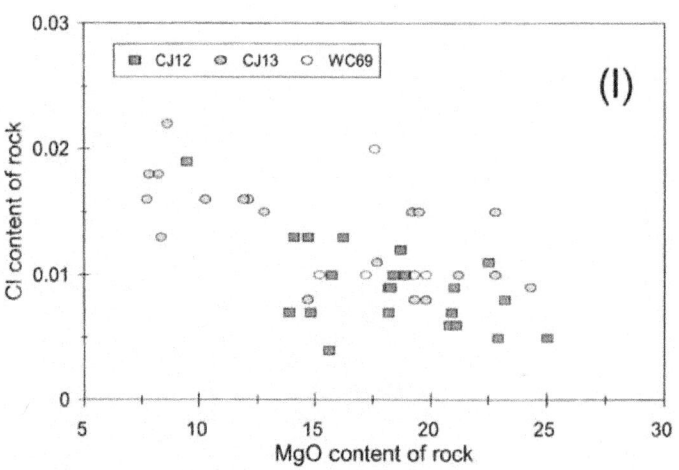

In accordance with prior observations (Helz and others, 1989), the migration of the minimum-density liquid has little effect on Al_2O_3 concentrations, because very little plagioclase has crystallized from the migrating liquid. Thus, in figure 9b most samples fall within or very near the field of olivine-controlled 1959 eruption compositions.

The effect on CaO is that the deeper, more olivine-rich (and hence more magnesian) regions of the lava lake, which have lost liquid by this process, are enriched in CaO relative to the array of 1959 eruption compositions, while samples from the upper parts of the lake (the receiving zone for the minimum-density liquid) are generally lower in CaO than eruption samples with comparable MgO contents. This is because the minimum-density liquid has crystallized significant augite, in addition to olivine (Helz and others, 1989). Hence the array of analyses in figure 9d cuts across the 1959 field, at a lower slope.

The effects of the melt-migration process on FeO (total) and TiO_2 are somewhat paradoxical, compared with classical models for tholeiitic fractionation, under which Fe and Ti both increase in the melt as fractionation proceeds. Because of reequilibration of olivine phenocrysts in the lower parts of the lake as temperature decreases (from an initial value of $1190\ ^{\circ}C$ to $\sim1160\ ^{\circ}C$ at plagioclase-in, as discussed in Helz and others, 1989; Helz, 2009), the migrating melt is depleted in FeO while being enriched in TiO_2, relative to eruption samples. These effects can be seen in figures 9e (total Fe as FeO) and 9f (TiO_2). The olivine-rich samples lie at higher FeO contents than the 1959 array and at lower TiO_2 contents. The low-MgO receiving zone shows the opposite signature. Variation in MnO (fig. 9g) tends to follow that of FeO, as manganese substitutes readily in olivine, especially as olivine becomes more iron-rich.

The various incompatible elements (Na_2O, K_2O, and P_2O_5) have patterns similar to that observed for TiO_2, as anticipated by Helz and others (1989). F and Cl follow P_2O_5, as the only phases in the basalt that can accommodate these three components are the melt and apatite. In general the concentrations of these elements are similar to those found by classical analysis (Helz and others, 1994). One peculiarity of the new results is that the F content for samples from job WC69 runs high relative to the other two analytical batches and the array of classical analyses (see fig. 7e in Helz and others, 1994).

Results for CO_2 and $H_2O\pm$

Analytical results for CO_2 show that its concentration is below the limit of detection (0.01 percent) in jobs CJ12 and CJ13, for all except two samples. The two exceptions (KI88-1-130.0 and KI88-1-138.4) were recovered from within the geothermal system in Kilauea Iki and may contain very minor carbonate. As discussed in Helz and others (1994), CO_2 is lost in pre- and syn-eruptive degassing. Therefore, samples from the lava lake, especially from this latest (1988) drilling, would be expected to contain no detectable magmatic CO_2, as was true for the analyses of earlier drill core.

The only phase in Kilauea Iki samples that can accommodate significant H_2O+ (structurally bound water) is the melt. Helz and others (1994) reported H_2O+ concentrations of 0.0–0.33 percent for H_2O+ in drill core, with over 70 percent of the samples having $H_2O+ > 0.02$ percent by weight. Although many of the samples in tables A1–A2 were quenched from high temperatures, and contain glass (quenched melt), few samples contain more than 20 percent melt. The maximum glass content in the 1988 core is ~25 percent by weight (in sample KI88-2-267.2, based on observed concentrations of K_2O and P_2O_5 in the interstitial glass), comparable to many earlier samples. The fact that H_2O+ was not detected in this or any other 1988 sample suggests that the H_2O+ content of the interstitial melt was lower in 1988 than the 0.05–0.15 percent by weight observed in the glassiest samples from 1967–1979 (Helz and others, 1994). Some samples in table A3 were quenched earlier and contain far more glass than the 1988 core; they might have significant H_2O+ , but neither CO_2 nor H_2O+ was determined for job WC69.

Determinations of H_2O- (adsorbed water) are very different in these analyses from the results for the classical analyses. Helz and others (1994) reported a range of 0.0–0.17 percent for H_2O-, with most samples having <0.02 percent by weight. By contrast, H_2O- values reported for samples from CJ12 range from 0.05–0.37 percent and in CJ13 range from 0.23–0.58 percent. Given that the summations for these batches exceed 100 percent even without the H_2O-, the H_2O- determinations would appear to be meaningless.

Discussion

The main purpose of this report is to show that the XRF data are sufficiently close to the classical analyses that the two sets can be treated as a unified body in evaluating fractionation in Kilauea Iki. Given that the two datasets are closely comparable, it is now possible to (1) describe the chemical variations of the 1988 drill core in the context of previously developed models for the differentiation of Kilauea Iki and (2) describe the chemical variations in the deeper parts of the lava lake, sampled only in 1988.

Most samples in tables A1–A3 were selected to be typical of their interval. The results in figures 9a–l show that the new analyses are broadly consistent with analyses of earlier (1960–1981) drill core and 1959 eruption samples. They are also consistent with the vertical chemical zonation described in Helz and others (1989). This chemical zonation is cryptic, with no mineralogical expression that can be seen in hand specimen, and overlays the gross zonation in olivine content discussed in Helz (1987a, 2009). Based on the 1960–1981 drill core, the lava lake was divided into five zones of different chemical character, depending on how core in the zones had been affected by processes other than olivine redistribution. Most samples in tables A1–A3 have been assigned to one or another of these five zones, as they show the same chemical characteristics as earlier core at the corresponding depths.

The two differentiation processes, each of which involves melt extraction and migration, are summarized in table 3 below. The first process (diapiric melt transfer) has grossly affected most of the lake between 40 and 310 ft (13 to 94 m). The receiving zone lies below 40 and above 160–170 ft (13 to ~50 m), while the source zone for this liquid begins at 190+ ft and extends to 310 ft (58–94 m), based on all available data. The "dead zone" that lies between these two regions, which was designated zone IV in Helz and others (1989), neither gave up nor received the minimum-density liquid.

The second process involves extraction of the Fe- and Ti-enriched ferrodiabasic liquid that forms the segregation veins. These veins occur as distinct internal differentiates within the upper crust, so there is no cryptic "receiving zone" as there is for the diapiric melt transfer

22

Table 3. Differentiation processes in Kilauea Iki lava lake (after table 1 in Helz, 2009). Depths rounded to whole meters.

	Differentiation Process	Depth range affected (meters)	Temperature range (ºC)
Processes occurring in molten core of lake, before formation of coherent crystal mush	Olivine settling	10 to 97+	>1180
	Lateral convection	20 to 43	1165 – 1170
	Diapiric melt transfer of minimum-density melt	13 to 94	1150 – 1160
Processes occurring within coherent crystal mush zones	Formation of ferrodiabasic segregation veins (coarse grained, sill-like, internal differentiates)	18 to 56	1100 – 1135
	Formation of vertical olivine-rich bodies (diapir tracks) that carried segregation vein melts through the lower part of the upper crust	18 to 58	<1140
	Formation of melt chimneys and speckled-rock plumes that carried differentiated melts upward from within lower mush zone in the lower crust	78 to 95	<1140

process. The chemical signature for extraction of this liquid occurs locally through much of the lake, especially in core below segregation veins: many samples in zone III and zone IV have lost some ferrodiabasic liquid (Helz and others, 1989) by this sort of local extraction. The extraction process itself is cryptic. However, most stages of migration of the lower-temperature, ferrodiabasic liquid leave discernible petrographic marks in the drill core, as summarized in table 3. These cross-cutting bodies are visibly enriched in differentiated, ferrodiabasic liquid relative to the adjacent matrix.

As anticipated in a note added to Helz and others (1989) in proof, results of the 1988 drilling allow the cryptic chemical stratigraphy of Kilauea Iki to be extended to greater depths. The deepest analyzed sample from the main body of the lake was formerly KI81-1-306.7, from 93.5 m (see fig. 3). However, tables A1 and A2 each contain eight analyses of samples recovered from below 300 ft and so offer insight into the deeper chemical stratigraphy of the main body of Kilauea Iki.

The overlapping effects of these two melt redistribution processes on Kilauea Iki, as sampled in the 1988 core, have produced a vertical chemical zonation, illustrated in figure 10, which can be summarized as follows:

(1) Relatively shallow samples from KI88-1 fall into zones II and III, which are enriched in minimum-density (1160 °C) liquid, with variable depletion in the ferrodiabasic liquid. As discussed in Helz (2009), core from KI88-1 is strongly enriched in the minimum-density liquid between the base of a block of foundered crust and the base of the olivine-depleted layer at 146 ft (44.5 m). The contact between zones II and III is at 146–147 ft in both 1988 cores (tables A1 and A2), consistent with its position in KI79-1 but somewhat deeper than in KI81-1.

(2) Zone IV, with samples either depleted in ferrodiabasic liquid or falling within the 1959 eruption compositional range, begins at 160–170 ft (49–52 m) in the 1988 cores, as in KI79-1, though deeper than found in KI81-1. Its base varies, lying at 195–205 ft (59–62 m) in the 1988 cores (tables A1–A2), which is somewhat deeper than observed in cores from KI79-1 and KI81-1.

(3) Zone V, depleted in only the minimum-density (1160 °C) liquid, was extensively discussed in Helz and others (1989) on the basis of data from cores KI81-1 and KI79-1. It has the same chemical character in cores KI88-2 and KI88-1; however, the top and base of this zone occur at somewhat greater depths in the 1988 cores (195–205 to 270 ft, or 58 to 82 m; see tables A1–A2) than in the earlier cores.

(4) Zone VI is depleted in both liquids. The existence of this zone was anticipated in Helz and others (1989) and was suggested by the character of the deepest samples from KI81-1. Samples from ~270 to 310 ft (82 to 94 m) in cores KI88-2 and KI88-1 also have this chemical signature, which suggests that this is indeed a lake-wide zone, with a lateral extent of at least 600 ft (see figs. 3 and 10).

(5) Zone VII, depleted in only the ferrodiabasic liquid, is intersected only in the 1988 cores. This zone is found in both KI88-2 and KI88-1 between 310 and 330 ft (94 to 99 m). Samples from this zone are some of the most extremely residual material in the lava lake, falling well outside the 1959 array in FeO (fig. 9e), TiO_2 (fig. 9f), and K_2O (fig. 9i); some are also unusually enriched in Al_2O_3 (fig. 9b) and CaO (fig. 9d) for their MgO contents.

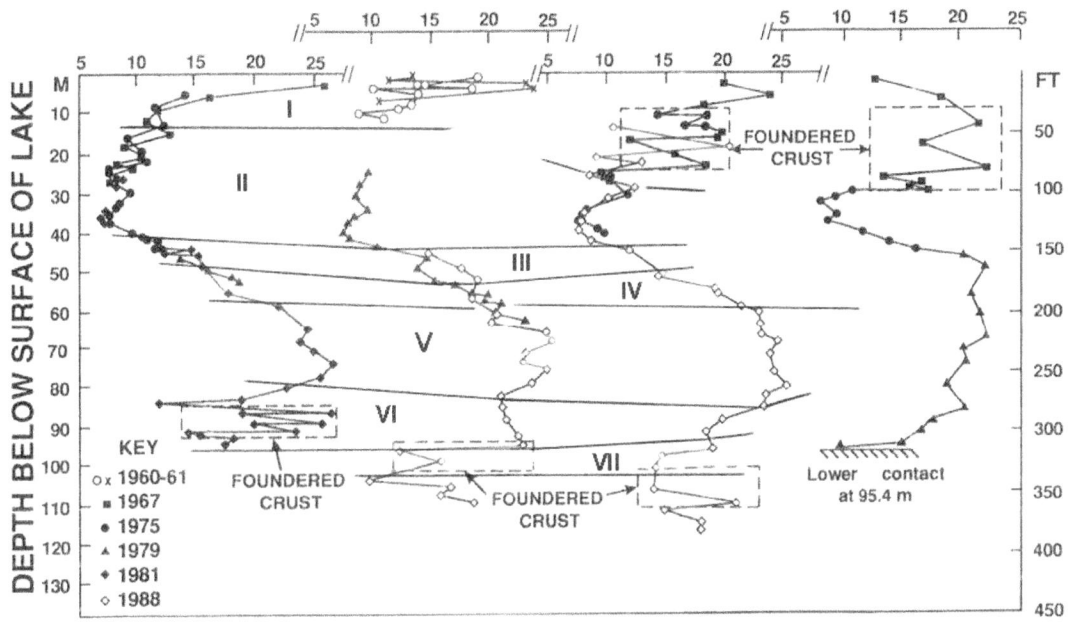

Figure 10. MgO content (weight percent) of olivine-phyric core versus depth below the surface of Kilauea Iki lava lake, after figure 3 in Helz (2009). Zone boundaries, as defined by the results of Helz and others (1994) and this report, are shown and the enclosed areas labeled as described in text.

Although zones VI and VII are depleted in ferrodiabasic liquid, there are no significant segregation veins at those depths. However, the 1988 cores locally contain melt chimneys and plumes of speckled rock [as described in Helz (1993) and indicated in table 3] over much of this depth range. These structures are interpreted as escape channels for differentiated liquid + bubbles; thus they are the lower-crust equivalent of the vertical olivine-rich bodies ("vorbs") that served as conduits for the ferrodiabasic liquid + bubbles in the upper crust (Helz, 1980; 1987a; Helz and others, 1989). Comparison of the depth intervals in table 3 with the zone assignments in tables A1–A2 shows that the plumes of speckled rock extend 3–10 ft (1–3 m) into zone V, beyond the top of zone VI. Similarly, most of zone VII lies below the region where there are well-developed plumes. Here, the core contains small irregular pods of segregation-vein material that did not coalesce into bodies large enough to rise. This offset in depth of plumes versus source zone for the melts is consistent with the inferred upward transport of ferrodiabasic liquid + bubbles.

The deepest samples from the 1988 cores fall within the 1959 eruption field in all components. Petrographically, they have moderate concentrations of olivine phenocrysts in a featureless, very dense groundmass. Samples from 260 to 300 ft in KI79-5 (just above the base of the lake at 313 ft; see fig. 3) also have moderate olivine phenocryst contents, a dense, featureless groundmass, and undifferentiated bulk chemistry. In that core, they are clearly samples of the lower chill zone of the lake. Given the similarity of the deepest 1988 samples, it appears that the 1988 holes also bottomed in the lower chill zone of Kilauea Iki. Based on the position of the maximum temperature in the 1988 holes, Helz (1993) estimated a minimum thickness for Kilauea Iki as ~427 ft (130 m). Because KI88-1 bottomed at 376 ft and KI88-2 at 355 ft, we are at least 55–75 ft (15–23 m) short of the lower contact of the 1959 lava lake. Nevertheless, the character of the deepest 1988 core samples suggests that the missing section will not be significantly differentiated. If this is true, we now have complete sections of the chemically differentiated central volume of Kilauea Iki.

Foundered Crust Versus the Vertical Zonation Pattern

The zone classification developed in Helz and others (1989) and extended here applies only to olivine-phyric "matrix rock," including the thin-bedded, highly variable "upper crust complex" (Helz, 1993) when it is found at 0–40 ft (0–12 m) in the lava lake. All internal differentiates having distinct boundaries with the matrix rock are excluded, as are some samples from blocks of foundered crust and their associated sheaths of undercooled material. In this report, samples of internal differentiates include two "vorbs" and one sample of a speckled-rock plume (all in table A1); they fall outside the overall zonation pattern and are not included in figure 10. Foundered crust and related samples are present in both 1988 cores, and such samples are identified in tables A1 and A2.

The locations of all major blocks of foundered crust encountered in drilling were first shown in Helz (1993) and are summarized here in figure 10. The most extensively sampled block is the material encountered in all cores from KI88-1 to the northernmost holes, interpreted to be a continuous wedge of foundered crust (Helz, 1993). This wedge thickens to the north with its base sloping down from 70 ft (21 m) in KI88-1 to 98 ft (30 m) in the KI79-5 cluster, as discussed in Helz (2009). This block was not affected by the longer range differentiation processes active in the rest of the lava lake (table 3).

By contrast, most samples from the three deep-seated blocks of foundered crust, found in cores from KI81-1 and KI81-5, in KI88-2, and in KI88-1, as shown in figure 10, have residual compositions appropriate to their depths. That is, they have lost the minimum-density liquid, the ferrodiabasic liquid, both, or neither, as follows:

(1) Most analyzed samples from the block intersected in the KI81-1 and KI81-5 cores have the doubly depleted signature of zone VI. Two of the denser samples within the block have zone V signatures, however; this suggests that the entire block participated in the higher temperature melt extraction, but only parts of the block subsequently lost the lower temperature ferrodiabasic liquid.

(2) Most samples from the block of foundered crust in KI88-2 have the chemical signatures of zone VI and VII (table A2; fig. 10). The sample immediately below the foundered crust has undifferentiated (1959) chemistry but is distinct in texture from the deepest samples, which are interpreted as lower chill zone.

(3) In KI88-1 (table A1; fig. 10), the foundered crust lies deeper than in the other two locations. In this core, the upper marginal sample has zone VII characteristics, but the rest of the block has undifferentiated (1959) chemistry.

Summary

This report presents 64 new major-element analyses for drill core from Kilauea Iki lava lake plus some related samples, obtained by X-ray fluorescence analysis during the period 1992 to 1995. Because earlier major-element data for the lava lake were gravimetric analyses (Helz and others, 1994), this report attempts to assess how well the two methods compare with each other, first by evaluating the results from samples that have been analyzed by both methods (tables A4a-g, figs. 8a-j). Then the new XRF analyses (tables A1-A3) have been evaluated as a group, using analytical summations and selected element ratios (figs. 5-8). These various evaluation methods suggest that the two sets of data are sufficiently close that they can be treated as a unified body in evaluating fractionation in Kilauea Iki.

Finally the new analyses have been plotted on magnesia variation diagrams (figs. 9a-l) and their variations compared with the field of 1959 eruption compositions (in itself a cross-check with earlier gravimetric data). The results show that the chemical variation of the 1988 core is consistent with that observed previously (Helz and others, 1989). Because the 1988 drilling recovered samples from greater depths than previous efforts, it has been possible to describe the chemical variations of the deeper parts of the lava lake and to extend the chemical zonation developed in Helz and others (1989) to greater depths. Lastly, the deepest samples from both 1988 drill cores appear, in olivine content, texture, and composition, to be like the lower chill zone samples from core KI79-5 (Helz and others, 1994). If they are samples of the lower chill zone in the center of the lava lake, then we now have two complete sections through the chemically differentiated part of Kilauea Iki lava lake.

References Cited

Barth, G.A., Kleinrock, M.C., and Helz, R.T., 1994, The magma body at Kilauea Iki lava lake, Potential insights into mid-ocean ridge magma chambers: Journal of Geophysical Research, v. 99, p. 7199–7217.

Eaton, J.P., Richter, D.H., and Krivoy, H.L., 1987, Cycling of magma between the summit reservoir and Kilauea Iki lava lake during the 1959 eruption of Kilauea Volcano, Chap. 48, *in* Decker, R.W., Wright, T.L., and Stauffer, P.H., eds., Volcanism in Hawaii: U.S. Geological Survey Professional Paper 1350, p. 1307–1336.

Flanagan, F.J., and Kirschenbaum, H., 1984, The precision of classical rock analysis: Geostandards Newsletter, v. 8, p. 7–11.

Helz, R.T., 1980, Crystallization history of Kilauea Iki lava lake as seen in drill core recovered in 1967–1979: Bulletin Volcanologique, v. 43–44, p. 675–701.

Helz, R.T., 1987a, Differentiation behavior of Kilauea Iki lava lake, Kilauea Volcano, Hawaii, An overview of past and current work, *in* Mysen, B.O., ed., Magmatic processes—Physicochemical principles: Geochemical Society Special Publication 1, p. 241–258.

Helz, R.T., 1987b, Diverse olivine types in lava of the 1959 eruption of Kilauea Volcano and their bearing on eruption dynamics, Chap. 25, *in* Decker, R.W., Wright, T.L., and Stauffer, P.H., eds., Volcanism in Hawaii: U.S. Geological Survey Professional Paper 1350, p. 691–722.

Helz, R.T., 1993, Drilling report and core logs for the 1988 drilling of Kilauea Iki lava lake, Kilauea Volcano, Hawaii, with summary descriptions of the occurrence of foundered crust and fractures in the drill core: U.S. Geological Survey Open-File Report 93–15, 57 p.

Helz, R.T., 2009, Processes active in mafic magma chambers, The example of Kilauea Iki lava lake, Hawaii: Lithos v. 111, p. 37–46.

Helz, R.T., Banks, N.G., Casadevall, T.J., Fiske, R.S., and Moore, R.B., 1984, A catalogue of drill core recovered from Kilauea Iki lava lake from 1967 to 1979: U.S. Geological Survey Open-File Report 84–484, 72 p.

Helz, R.T., Kirschenbaum, H.K., and Marinenko, J.W., 1989, Diapiric transfer of melt in Kilauea Iki lava lake, Hawaii—A quick, efficient process of igneous differentiation: Geological Society of America Bulletin, v. 101, p. 578–594.

Helz, R.T., Kirschenbaum, H.K., Marinenko, J.W., and Qian, Rachel, 1994, Whole-rock analyses of core samples from the 1967, 1975, 1979 and 1981 drillings of Kilauea Iki Lava Lake, Hawaii: U.S. Geological Survey Open-File Report 94–684, 65 p.

Helz, R.T., and Thornber, C.R., 1987, Geothermometry of Kilauea Iki lava lake: Bulletin of Volcanology, v. 49, p. 651–668.

Helz, R.T., and Wright, T.L., 1983, Drilling report and core logs for the 1981 drilling of Kilauea Iki lava lake (Kilauea Volcano, Hawaii), with comparative notes on earlier (1967–1979) drilling experiences: U.S. Geological Survey Open-File Report 83–326, 66 p.

Jackson, L.L., Brown, F.W., and Neil, S.T., 1987, Major and minor elements requiring individual determination, classical whole rock analysis, and rapid rock analysis, *in* Baedecker, P.A., ed., Methods for geochemical analysis: U.S. Geological Survey Bulletin 1770, p. G1–G23.

Kirschenbaum, Herbert, 1983, The classical chemical analysis of silicate rocks—The old and the new: U.S. Geological Survey Bulletin 1547, 55 p.

Kirschenbaum, Herbert, 1988, The determination of fluoride in silicate rocks by ion-selective electrode, An update: U.S. Geological Survey Open-File Report 88–588, 5 p.

Lichte, F.D., Golightly, D.W., and Lamothe, P.J., 1987, Inductively coupled plasma-atomic emission spectrometry, in Baedecker, P.A. ed., Methods for geochemical analysis: U.S. Geological Survey Bulletin 1770, p. B1–B10.

Murata, K.J., and Richter, D.H., 1966, Chemistry of the lavas of the 1959–60 eruption of Kilauea Volcano, Hawaii: U.S. Geological Survey Professional Paper 537–A, 26 p.

Peck, L.C., 1964, Systematic analysis of silicates: U.S. Geological Survey Bulletin 1170, 89 p.

Pitcher, L., Helz, R.T., Walker, R.J., and Piccoli, P., 2009, Fractionation of the platinum-group elements and Re during crystallization of basalt in Kilauea Iki lava lake, Hawaii:. Chemical Geology, v. 260, p. 196–210.

Richter, D.H., Eaton, J.P., Murata, K.J., Ault, W.U., and Krivoy, H.L., 1970, Chronologic narrative of the 1959–1960 eruption of Kilauea Volcano, Hawaii: U.S. Geological Survey Professional Paper 537–E, 73 p.

Richter, D.H., and Moore, J.G., 1966, Petrology of the Kilauea Iki lava lake, Hawaii: U.S. Geological Survey Professional Paper 537–B, 26 p.

Taggart, J.E., Jr., Lindsey, J.R., Scott, B.A., Vivit, D.V., Bartell, A.J., and Stewart, K.C., 1987, Analysis of geologic materials by wavelength dispersive X-ray fluorescence spectrometry, in Baedecker, P.A., ed., Methods for geochemical analysis: U.S. Geological Survey Bulletin 1770, p. E1–E19.

Taggart, J.E., Jr., and Siems, D.R., 2002, Major element analysis by wavelength dispersive X-ray fluorescence spectrometry, Chap. T, in Taggart, J.E., Jr., ed., Analytical methods for chemical analysis of geologic and other materials: U.S. Geological Survey Open-File Report 02–0223–T, 9 p.

Taylor, C.F., and Theodorakos, P.M., 2002, Sample preparation, in Taggart, J.E., Jr., ed., Analytical methods for chemical analysis of geologic and other materials: U.S. Geological Survey Open-File Report 02–0223–A1, 5 p.

Teng, F.-Z., Dauphas, Nicolas, and Helz, R.T., 2008, Iron isotope fractionation during magmatic differentiation in Kilauea Iki Lava Lake: Science, v. 320, p.1620–1622.

Teng, F.-Z., Wadhwa, M., and Helz, R.T., 2007, Investigation of magnesium isotope fractionation during basalt differentiation: Implications for a chondritic composition of the terrestrial mantle: Earth and Planetary Science Letters, v. 261, p. 84–92.

Thornber, C.R., Sherrod, D.R., Siems, D.F., Heliker, C.C., Meeker, G.P., Oscarson, R.L., and Kauahikaua, J.P., 2002, Whole-rock and glass major-element geochemistry of Kilauea Volcano, Hawaii, near vent eruptive products, September 1994 through September 2001: U.S. Geological Survey Open-File Report 2002–017, 9 p.

Wright, T.L., 1971, Chemistry of Kilauea and Mauna Loa lava in space and time: U.S. Geological Survey Professional Paper 735, 40 p.

Wright, T.L., 1973, Magma mixing as illustrated by the 1959 eruption, Kilauea Volcano, Hawaii: Geological Society of America Bulletin, v. 84, p. 849–858.

Wright, T.L., and Fiske, R.S., 1971, Origin of the differentiated and hybrid lavas of Kilauea Volcano, Hawaii: Journal of Petrology, v. 12, p. 1–65.

Table A1. X-ray fluorescence analyses of core from Kilauea Iki drill hole KI88-1, in weight percent. Numbers in italics not included in totals. Sample annotations as discussed in text.

	1	2	3	4	5	6	7	8
Field No.	KI88-1-41.4	KI88-1-60.4	KI88-1-66.9	KI88-1-73.4	KI88-1-84.3	KI88-1-94.1	KI88-1-102.2	KI88-1-111.9
Lab no.	D-571891	D-571892	D-571893	W-256752	W-256753	W-256754	W-256755	W-256756
Job no.	WC69	WC69	WC69	CJ13	CJ13	CJ13	CJ13	CJ13
SiO_2	47.8	46.1	49.4	48.5	49.8	48.9	49.3	50.4
Al_2O_3	11.7	8.88	12.8	11.6	13.0	11.9	12.3	13.2
Fe_2O_3	4.75	0.95	1.85	1.57	2.29	1.98	2.30	2.27
FeO	8.24	11.3	9.59	10.2	9.1	9.2	9.0	8.4
MgO	10.4	20.6	8.91	12.8	8.36	12.1	10.3	8.24
CaO	10.3	8.25	11.1	10.2	10.8	10.1	10.3	10.5
Na_2O	2.13	1.43	2.23	1.87	2.30	2.06	2.19	2.44
K_2O	0.55	0.31	0.55	0.49	0.60	0.53	0.58	0.69
H_2O+	--	--	--	<0.01	<0.01	<0.01	<0.01	<0.01
H_2O-	*--*	*--*	*--*	*(0.51)*	*(0.34)*	*(0.26)*	*(0.25)*	*(0.41)*
TiO_2	3.00	1.47	2.63	2.49	3.09	2.61	2.89	3.03
P_2O_5	0.28	0.18	0.31	0.26	0.30	0.28	0.31	0.36
MnO	0.18	0.18	0.17	0.17	0.17	0.17	0.17	0.16
CO_2	--	--	--	<0.01	<0.01	<0.01	<0.01	<0.01
Cl	<.01	<.01	<.01	.015	.013	.016	.016	.018
F	0.06	0.04	0.07	.030	.040	.034	.020	.031
Cr_2O_3	0.06	0.18	0.04	0.10	0.05	0.11	0.09	0.07
Subtotal	99.45	99.87	99.65	100.29	99.92	99.99	99.76	99.81
Less O=Cl,F	.02	.01	.02	.02	.02	.02	.02	.02
Total	99.43	99.86	99.63	100.27	99.90	99.97	99.74	99.79
Type of sample (zone)	adjacent to foundered crust	foundered crust	adjacent to foundered crust	adjacent to foundered crust	(II)	(II)	(II)	(II)
Contains glass?	no	no	no	no	no	no	no	no
Temperature before quench	low	low	low	low	low	low	low	low

30

Table A1. Analyses of core from drill hole KI88-1 (continued).

	9	10	11	12	13	14	15
Field no.	KI88-1-123.6	KI88-1-130.0	KI88-1-138.4	KI88-1-146.4	KI88-1-156.4	KI88-1-156.7	KI88-1-164.3
Lab. no.	W-256757	W-256758	W-256759	W-256760	D-571894	W256761	W-256762
Job no.	CJ13	CJ13	CJ13	CJ13	WC69	CJ13	CJ13
SiO_2	50.3	50.5	50.0	49.0	46.8	46.7	48.3
Al_2O_3	13.3	13.1	12.8	11.7	9.33	9.48	11.6
Fe_2O_3	2.58	2.70	2.67	2.17	1.31	1.83	1.82
FeO	8.3	8.1	8.4	9.3	10.70	10.5	8.8
MgO	7.74	7.82	8.64	11.9	18.5	19.3	14.7
CaO	10.7	10.4	10.4	10.1	8.84	8.62	10.5
Na_2O	2.44	2.51	2.38	2.07	1.53	1.38	1.67
K_2O	0.67	0.72	0.66	0.53	0.38	0.36	0.38
H_2O+	<0.01	<0.01	<0.01	<0.01	--	<0.01	<0.01
H_2O-	(0.43)	(0.58)	(0.48)	(0.33)	--	(0.32)	(0.29)
TiO_2	3.22	3.34	3.30	2.64	1.84	1.67	1.98
P_2O_5	0.35	0.37	0.35	0.29	0.22	0.19	0.21
MnO	0.16	0.16	0.16	0.17	0.17	0.18	0.16
CO_2	<0.01	0.08	0.02	<0.01	--	<0.01	<0.01
Cl	.016	.018	.022	.016	<.01	.008	.008
F	.040	.043	.041	.030	0.05	.024	.022
Cr_2O_3	0.06	0.06	0.07	0.12	0.15	0.18	0.16
Subtotal	99.88	99.93	99.91	100.03	99.82	100.42	100.32
Less O=Cl,F	.02	.02	.02	.02	.02	.01	.01
Total	99.86	99.91	99.89	100.01	99.80	100.41	100.31
Type of sample (zone)	(II)	(II)	(II)	(II/III)	vorb	vorb	(IV)
Contains glass?	no	no	no	no	no	no	no
Temperature before quench	low	low	low	low	low	low	low

31

Table A1. Analyses of core from drill hole KI88-1 (continued).

	16	17	18	19	20	21	22	23
Field no.	KI88-1-165.0	KI88-1-172.2	KI88-1-182.3	KI88-1-190.7	KI88-1-198.6	KI88-1-205.4	KI88-1-213.7	KI88-1-222.5
Lab. no.	D-571895	D-571896	W-256763	W-256764	W-256765	W-256766	W-256736	W-256767
Job no.	WC69	WC69	CJ13	CJ13	CJ13	CJ13	CJ12	CJ13
SiO_2	48.1	46.4	46.7	46.4	45.9	45.8	45.5	45.2
Al_2O_3	11.2	9.07	9.57	8.86	8.34	8.30	8.20	7.63
Fe_2O_3	1.42	1.21	1.99	1.65	1.07	1.72	1.18	1.45
FeO	9.07	10.7	10.0	10.4	11.1	10.6	11.0	11.3
MgO	14.5	19.3	19.2	21.2	22.8	22.8	22.9	24.3
CaO	10.5	9.15	9.11	8.52	8.17	8.12	8.10	7.36
Na_2O	1.78	1.36	1.34	1.24	1.12	1.09	1.08	1.04
K_2O	0.41	0.29	0.31	0.30	0.26	0.26	0.26	0.25
H_2O+	--	--	<0.01	<0.01	<0.01	<0.01	<0.01	<0.01
H_2O-	--	--	*(0.45)*	*(0.57)*	*(0.32)*	*(0.27)*	*(0.18)*	*(0.36)*
TiO_2	2.02	1.56	1.62	1.48	1.48	1.35	1.35	1.31
P_2O_5	0.23	0.18	0.17	0.16	0.16	0.16	0.15	0.15
MnO	0.16	0.18	0.18	0.18	0.18	0.18	0.18	0.19
CO_2	--	--	.01	.01	<0.01	<0.01	<0.01	<0.01
Cl	<.01	<.01	.015	.010	.010	.015	.005	.009
F	0.05	0.04	.021	.014	.020	.020	.006	.020
Cr_2O_3	0.14	0.16	0.20	0.24	0.26	0.23	0.25	0.23
Subtotal	99.58	99.60	100.44	100.66	100.76	100.65	100.16	100.44
Less O=Cl,F	.02	.01	.01	.01	.01	.01	.00	.01
Total	99.56	99.59	100.43	100.65	100.75	100.64	100.16	100.43
Type of sample (zone)	(IV)	(IV)	(IV)	(IV)	(V)	(V)	(V)	(V)
Contains glass?	no	no	no	no	no	no	no	no
Temperature before quench	low	low	low	low	low	low	low	low

Table A1. Analyses of core from drill hole KI88-1 (continued).

	24	25	26	27	28	29	30
Field no.	KI88-1-234.4	KI88-1-249.1	KI88-1-260.0	KI88-1-268.5	KI88-1-277.8	KI88-1-288.6	KI88-1-298.3
Lab. no.	W256737	W-256738	W-256739	W-256740	W-256741	W-256768	W-256742
Job no.	CJ12	CJ12	CJ12	CJ12	CJ12	CJ13	CJ12
SiO_2	45.5	45.2	45.1	45.7	45.5	46.5	47.2
Al_2O_3	8.06	7.81	7.62	8.22	8.23	9.38	9.88
Fe_2O_3	0.96	1.58	1.58	1.90	1.50	1.98	1.45
FeO	11.2	11.0	11.0	10.8	10.8	10.1	10.4
MgO	23.8	24.1	25.0	23.2	23.2	19.5	18.2
CaO	8.10	7.93	7.27	7.10	8.22	8.74	8.93
Na_2O	1.04	0.95	0.99	1.24	1.03	1.33	1.52
K_2O	0.23	0.22	0.24	0.32	0.23	0.32	0.39
H_2O+	<0.01	<0.01	<0.01	<0.01	<0.01	<0.01	<0.01
H_2O-	(0.16)	(0.20)	(0.13)	(0.15)	(0.20)	(0.23)	(0.11)
TiO_2	1.22	1.17	1.17	1.55	1.18	1.63	1.88
P_2O_5	0.14	0.14	0.14	0.18	0.13	0.19	0.21
MnO	0.18	0.19	0.18	0.18	0.18	0.18	0.18
CO_2	<0.01	<0.01	<0.01	<0.01	<0.01	<0.01	<0.01
Cl	<.004	<.004	.005	.008	.008	.015	.009
F	.012	.010	.010	.020	.008	.030	.020
Cr_2O_3	0.25	0.27	0.26	0.22	0.27	0.20	0.19
Subtotal	100.69	100.57	100.56	100.64	100.48	100.09	100.46
Less O=Cl,F	.00	.00	.01	.01	.01	.02	.01
Total	100.69	100.57	100.55	100.63	100.47	100.07	100.45
Type of sample (zone)	(V)	(V)	(V)	speckled rock body	nearest Tmax (V)	(VI)	(VI)
Contains glass?	no	yes	yes	yes	yes	yes	yes
Temperature before quench	medium	high	high	high	high	high	high

33

Table A1. Analyses of core from drill hole KI88-1 (continued).

	31	32	33	34	35	36	37	38
Field no.	KI88-1-311.6	KI88-1-317.7	KI88-1-329.1	KI88-1-347.3	KI88-1-358.2	KI88-1-362.5	KI88-1-371.2	KI88-1-375.8
Lab. no.	W-256743	D-571897	W-256744	W-256745	W-256746	W256747	W-256748	W-256749
Job no.	CJ12	WC69	CJ12	CJ12	CJ12	CJ12	CJ12	CJ12
SiO_2	47.0	47.7	48.2	48.2	46.3	47.8	47.1	47.0
Al_2O_3	9.72	11.1	11.6	11.5	8.98	11.3	9.82	9.76
Fe_2O_3	1.35	1.46	1.06	1.45	1.75	2.27	1.46	1.99
FeO	10.4	9.76	10.3	10.4	10.4	9.3	10.3	10.0
MgO	18.7	15.2	14.1	13.9	21.0	14.7	18.4	18.3
CaO	8.61	9.94	10.1	9.97	7.79	9.84	8.77	8.68
Na_2O	1.52	1.77	1.77	1.75	1.38	1.72	1.55	1.51
K_2O	0.39	0.35	0.40	0.43	0.37	0.41	0.40	0.39
H_2O+	<.01	--	<0.01	<0.01	<0.01	<0.01	<0.01	<0.01
H_2O-	*(0.09)*	--	*(0.37)*	*(0.29)*	*(0.27)*	*(0.31)*	*(0.19)*	*(0.21)*
TiO_2	1.85	1.82	2.03	2.09	1.81	2.13	1.92	1.98
P_2O_5	0.23	0.21	0.21	0.23	0.20	0.23	0.22	0.22
MnO	0.17	0.17	0.17	0.18	0.18	0.17	0.17	0.17
CO_2	<0.01	--	<0.01	<0.01	<0.01	<0.01	<0.01	<0.01
Cl	.012	.01	.013	.007	.009	.013	.010	.009
F	.022	.07	.022	.022	.012	.020	.011	.030
Cr_2O_3	0.20	0.12	0.13	0.13	0.23	0.15	0.20	0.20
Subtotal	100.17	99.68	100.11	100.25	100.41	100.05	100.33	100.24
Less O=Cl,F	.01	.00	.02	.01	.01	.02	.01	.01
Total	100.16	99.68	100.09	100.24	100.40	100.03	100.32	100.23
Type of sample (zone)	(VII)	(VII)	adjacent to foundered crust (VII)	foundered crust	foundered crust	adjacent to foundered crust	chill	deepest core - chill
Contains glass?	yes	yes	yes	no	no	no	no	no
Temperature before quench	high	high	high	medium	medium	medium	medium	medium

34

Table A2. X-ray fluorescence analyses of core from Kilauea Iki drill hole KI88-2, in weight percent. Numbers in italics not included in totals. Sample annotations discussed in text.

	1	2	3	4	5	6	7	8
Field no.	KI88-2-147.4	KI88-2-160.5	KI88-2-170.2	KI88-2-177.2	KI88-2-186.7	KI88-2-197.7	KI88-2-205.2	KI88-2-215.8
Lab. no.	W-256718	W-256750	W-256719	D-571898	W-256720	W-256721	W-256751	W-256722
Job no.	CJ12	CJ13	CJ12	WC69	CJ12	CJ12	CJ13	CJ12
SiO2	48.0	47.3	46.7	46.8	47.1	46.5	46.7	45.3
Al2O3	11.0	10.1	9.54	10.1	10.1	9.21	9.45	7.83
Fe2O3	2.06	2.76	1.87	1.29	1.26	1.45	1.62	1.70
FeO	9.4	9.4	10.2	10.0	10.3	10.4	9.7	10.8
MgO	14.8	17.7	18.9	17.6	17.9	20.4	19.8	24.3
CaO	9.85	9.16	8.99	9.55	9.61	8.94	9.35	7.76
Na2O	1.71	1.53	1.40	1.52	1.54	1.28	1.28	1.01
K2O	0.43	0.37	0.34	0.33	0.36	0.30	0.31	0.24
H2O+	<0.01	<0.01	<0.01	--	<0.01	<0.01	<0.01	<0.01
H2O-	*(0.10)*	*(0.43)*	*(0.12)*	*--*	*(0.11)*	*(0.21)*	*(0.36)*	*(0.18)*
TiO2	2.25	1.90	1.70	1.68	1.70	1.53	1.54	1.21
P2O5	0.23	0.20	0.19	0.20	0.19	0.17	0.17	0.14
MnO	0.17	0.18	0.18	0.17	0.17	0.18	0.17	0.18
CO2	<0.01	<0.01	<0.01	--	<0.01	<0.01	0.01	<0.01
Cl	.007	.011	.010	.02	.085	<.004	.008	<.004
F	.013	.020	.020	.05	.020	.011	.012	.008
Cr2O3	0.14	0.16	0.19	0.14	0.19	0.21	0.21	0.26
Subtotal	100.06	100.79	100.23	99.45	100.52	100.58	100.32	100.74
Less O=Cl,F	.01	.01	.01	.00	.04	.00	.01	.00
Total	100.05	100.78	100.22	99.45	100.48	100.58	100.31	100.74
Type of sample (zone)	(II/III)	(III)	(III/IV)	(IV)	(IV)	(IV)	(IV)	(V)
Contains glass?	no	no	no	no	no	no	no	no
Temperature before quench	low	low	low	low	low	low	low	medium

35

Table A2. Analyses of core from drill hole KI88-2 (continued).

	9	10	11	12	13	14	15	16
Field no.	KI88-2-224.3	KI88-2-231.8	KI88-2-242.1	KI88-2-249.7	KI88-2-256.4	KI88-2-267.2	KI88-2-276.3	KI88-2-287.6
Lab. no.	D-571899	W-256723	D-571900	W-256724	W-256725	W-256726	W-256727	W-256728
Job no.	WC69	CJ12	WC69	CJ12	CJ12	CJ12	CJ12	CJ12
SiO2	45.0	45.6	45.9	45.2	45.4	46.1	46.1	46.3
Al2O3	7.39	8.25	8.85	7.92	8.26	9.00	9.37	9.39
Fe2O3	1.23	1.40	1.33	1.28	1.57	1.70	1.19	1.55
FeO	11.4	10.8	10.5	11.0	11.1	10.8	10.9	10.4
MgO	24.5	22.8	21.4	24.6	23.4	20.91	20.8	21.1
CaO	7.33	8.22	8.64	8.07	7.73	7.97	8.53	8.61
Na2O	1.06	1.07	1.22	0.92	1.09	1.35	1.28	1.24
K2O	0.24	0.26	0.26	0.29	0.25	0.33	0.27	0.27
H2O+	--	<0.01	--	<0.01	<.01	<.01	<0.01	<.01
H2O-	--	*(0.18)*	--	*(0.07)*	*(0.18)*	*(0.14)*	*(0.07)*	*(0.06)*
TiO2	1.24	1.31	1.28	1.00	1.24	1.62	1.35	1.34
P2O5	0.15	0.15	0.16	0.12	0.15	0.19	0.15	0.15
MnO	0.18	0.18	0.17	0.18	0.18	0.18	0.18	0.18
CO2	--	<0.01	--	<0.01	<0.01	<0.01	<0.01	<0.01
Cl	<.01	<.004	<.01	<.004	<.004	.007	.006	.006
F	.03	.007	.04	.005	.007	.013	.008	.010
Cr2O3	0.21	0.25	0.18	0.26	0.23	0.20	0.21	0.22
Subtotal	99.96	100.30	99.93	100.75	100.60	100.28	100.35	100.76
Less O=Cl,F	.01	.00	.01	.00	.00	.01	.00	.01
Total	99.95	100.30	99.92	100.75	100.60	100.27	100.35	100.75
Type of sample (zone)	(V)	(V)	(V)	(V)	(V)	at T(max) (V)	(VI)	(VI)
Contains glass?	no	no	yes	yes	yes	yes	yes	yes
Temperature before quench	medium	medium	high	high	high	high	high	high

36

Table A2. Analyses of core from drill hole KI88-2 (continued).

	17	18	19	20	21	22	23	24
Field no.	KI88-2-301.7	KI88-2-309.2	KI88-2-316.2	KI88-2-322.3	KI88-2-336.3	KI88-2-343.7	KI88-2-348.5	KI88-2-354.9
Lab no.	W-256729	W-256730	D-571901	W-256731	W-256732	W-256733	W-256734	W-256735
Job no.	CJ12	CJ12	WC69	CJ12	CJ12	CJ12	CJ12	CJ12
SiO_2	45.8	46.3	49.1	48.0	49.7	47.5	47.7	47.1
Al_2O_3	8.98	8.66	13.5	11.7	12.5	10.6	10.7	9.83
Fe_2O_3	1.07	1.32	1.73	1.15	1.81	2.53	1.67	1.55
FeO	11.1	10.6	7.53	9.5	8.9	9.6	10.2	10.4
MgO	22.1	22.5	10.7	15.6	9.49	16.2	15.7	18.2
CaO	8.45	7.17	12.3	10.6	11.7	9.09	9.23	8.75
Na_2O	1.19	1.38	2.01	1.69	2.03	1.67	1.73	1.54
K_2O	0.18	0.40	0.32	0.25	0.53	0.44	0.44	0.40
H_2O+	<0.01	<0.01	--	<0.01	<0.01	<0.01	<0.01	<0.01
H_2O-	*(0.08)*	*(0.08)*	--	*(0.06)*	*(0.08)*	*(0.07)*	*(0.05)*	*(0.05)*
TiO_2	1.10	1.53	1.64	1.44	2.74	2.12	2.22	1.96
P_2O_5	0.11	0.22	0.17	0.14	0.27	0.23	0.23	0.22
MnO	0.18	0.17	0.15	0.16	0.16	0.18	0.16	0.18
CO_2	<0.01	<0.01	--	<0.01	<0.01	<0.01	<0.01	<0.01
Cl	<.004	.011	<.01	.004	.019	.013	.010	.007
F	.006	.020	.04	.011	.030	.020	.030	.013
Cr_2O_3	0.24	0.20	0.07	0.18	0.08	0.15	0.14	0.19
Subtotal	100.51	100.48	99.26	100.42	99.96	100.35	100.17	100.34
Less O=Cl,F	.00	.01	.00	.00	.02	.01	.01	.01
Total	100.51	100.47	99.26	100.42	99.94	100.34	100.16	100.33
Type of sample (zone)	adjacent to foundered crust (VI)	foundered crust (VI)	foundered crust (VII)	foundered crust (VII)	adjacent to foundered crust	chill	chill	deepest core - chill
Contains glass?	yes	yes	yes	yes	yes	no	no	no
Temperature before quench	high	high	high	high	high	medium	medium	medium

37

Table A3. X-ray fluorescence analyses of samples from drill hole KI79-1, plus the 1959 and 1960 eruptions of Kilauea, in weight percent.

	1	2	3	4	5	6
Field no.	KI79-1-183.4	KI79-1-187.4	Iki-3	Iki-14	Iki-14	KP-16
Lab. no.	D-571902	D-571903	D-571889	D-571888	In PP537-A	D-571890
Job no.	WC69	WC69	WC69	WC69		WC69
Analysis type	XRF	XRF	XRF	XRF	rapid-rock	XRF
SiO_2	46.3	46.3	47.2	46.9	46.7	49.6
Al_2O_3	8.80	9.32	9.87	9.65	10.0	12.8
Fe_2O_3	1.40	1.20	2.41	1.60	1.5	1.79
FeO	10.8	10.6	9.44	10.2	10.4	9.91
MgO	19.8	19.3	17.2	18.1	18.2	8.71
CaO	8.67	8.60	8.95	8.48	8.3	10.0
Na_2O	1.40	1.46	1.67	1.63	1.9	2.40
K_2O	0.33	0.34	0.41	0.41	0.40	0.61
H_2O+	–	–	–	–	–	–
H_2O-	–	–	–	–	–	–
TiO_2	1.65	1.66	2.01	1.99	1.9	2.88
P_2O_5	0.20	0.20	0.24	0.23	0.22	0.35
MnO	0.18	0.17	0.17	0.17	0.17	0.17
CO_2	–	–	–	–	–	–
Cl	.01	.01	.01	<.01	–	.01
F	.04	.04	.04	.05	–	.09
Cr_2O_3	0.16	0.16	0.16	0.16	–	0.05
Subtotal	99.74	99.36	99.78	99.57	99.69	99.37
Less O=Cl,F	.02	.02	.02	.02	.02	.04
Total	99.72	99.34	99.76	99.55	99.67	99.35
Type of sample	above overnight stop (184.4)	below overnight stop (184.4)	1959 phase 1	1959 phase 5	1959 phase 5	1960 late hybrid
Contains glass?	yes	yes	yes	yes	yes	yes
Temperature	high	high	high	high	high	high

Table A4a. X-ray fluorescence analyses of core from drill hole KI67-1 compared with gravimetric analyses, all in weight percent. Sample annotations as in Helz and others (1994).

	1	2	3	4	5	6
Field no.	KI67-1-9.5	KI67-1-9.5	KI67-1-17.1	KI67-1-17.1	KI67-1-54.9	KI67-1-54.9
Lab. no.	W-232722	W-232722	W-232723	W-232723	D-102044	D-102044
Job no.		BR98		BR98		955(DCS)
Analysis type	XRF	gravimetric	XRF	gravimetric	XRF	gravimetric
SiO2	46.39	46.42	45.22	45.24	48.93	49.05
Al2O3	9.38	9.37	7.95	7.90	11.73	11.95
Fe2O3 (total)	13.01	12.89	13.35	13.20	12.83	12.80
FeO	--	--	--		--	
MgO	19.77	19.63	24.28	24.14	11.85	11.73
CaO	7.99	8.23	6.78	6.89	9.34	9.41
Na2O	1.51	1.47	1.21	1.23	2.09	2.19
K2O	0.38	.35	0.31	0.29	0.69	0.69
H2O+	--	.07	--	.01	--	.21
H2O-	--	.07	--	.10	--	.00
TiO2	1.89	1.89	1.51	1.51	2.66	2.69
P2O5	0.20	.19	0.16	0.16	0.36	0.32
MnO	0.17	.17	0.18	0.17	0.17	0.17
CO2	--	.01	--	.01	--	.01
Cl	--	.005	--	.008	--	.026
F	--	.023	--	.024	--	.038
Cr2O3	--	0.19	--	0.21	--	--
Type of sample					leopard rock	leopard rock
Contains glass?	no	no	no	no	no	no
Temperature before quench	low	low	low	low	medium	medium

39

Table A4b. X-ray fluorescence analyses of core from drill holes KI67-2 and KI79-5, compared with gravimetric analyses, all in weight percent. Sample annotations as in Helz and others (1994). "XRF recheck" indicates sample re-analyzed for cause, as discussed in text.

	1	2	3	4	5	6	7
Field no.	KI67-2-0.5	KI67-2-0.5	KI67-2-17.0	KI67-2-40.4	KI67-2-40.4	KI67-2-59.8	KI79-5-180.9
Lab. no.	W-232721	W-232721	W-256769	W-214300	W-214300	W-256770	W-256771
Job no.		BR98	CJ13		BD25	CJ13	CJ13
Analysis type	XRF	gravimetric	XRF recheck	XRF	wet chem.	XRF recheck	XRF recheck
SiO2	48.20	48.23	46.9	45.96	45.71	47.7	46.2
Al2O3	11.64	12.32	9.96	8.92	8.94	10.7	9.05
Fe2O3 (total)	12.57	12.20	13.1	13.40	13.19	12.6	12.9
FeO	--	--	--	--	--	--	--
MgO	12.68	12.58	18.5	21.65	21.77	16.7	20.8
CaO	10.20	10.37	8.56	7.66	7.64	9.11	8.55
Na2O	1.89	1.85	1.55	1.36	1.50	1.70	1.29
K2O	0.48	0.44	0.38	0.31	0.32	0.43	0.31
H2O+	--	.08	--	--	.00	--	--
H2O-	--	.10	--	--	.04	--	--
TiO2	2.32	2.30	1.87	1.64	1.49	2.06	1.57
P2O5	0.24	0.26	0.21	0.17	0.14	0.23	0.18
MnO	0.17	0.17	0.18	0.18	0.18	0.17	0.17
CO2	--	<0.01	--	--	.01	--	--
Cl	--	.011	--	--	.003	--	--
F	--	.030	--	--	.021	--	--
Cr2O3	--	0.12	--	--	0.19	--	--
Type of sample							
Contains glass?	no	no	no	no	no	no	yes
Temperature before quench	low	low	low	medium	medium	medium	high

Table A4c. X-ray fluorescence analyses of core from drill hole KI67-3 compared with gravimetric analyses, all in weight percent. Sample annotations as in Helz and others (1994).

	1	2	3	4	5	6	7	8
Field no.	KI67-3-74.0	KI67-3-74.0	KI67-3-76.2	KI67-3-76.2	KI67-3-78.3	KI67-3-78.3	KI67-3-83.8	KI67-3-83.8
Lab. no.	D-103982	D-103982	D-102053	D-102053	D-103983	D-103983	D-103986	D-103986
Job no.		PH48		955(DCS)		PH48		PH48
Analysis type	XRF	gravimetric	XRF	gravimetric	XRF	gravimetric	XRF	gravimetric
SiO_2	49.98	49.81	50.77	50.82	49.67	49.66	50.17	49.93
Al_2O_3	13.25	13.60	12.30	12.72	13.14	13.32	13.24	13.61
Fe_2O_3 (total)	11.69	11.55	14.11	14.15	12.19	12.19	12.15	12.12
FeO	--		--		--		--	
MgO	8.36	8.27	5.15	5.14	8.03	7.90	7.63	7.54
CaO	11.23	11.37	9.17	9.34	10.86	11.00	10.77	10.80
Na_2O	2.29	2.40	2.82	2.90	2.33	2.43	2.43	2.46
K_2O	0.59	0.60	0.99	1.00	0.60	0.60	0.66	0.67
H_2O+	--	.12	--	.20	--	.12	--	.14
H_2O-	--	.01	--	.00	--	.01	--	.01
TiO_2	2.87	2.82	4.40	4.34	3.09	3.06	3.06	2.99
P_2O_5	0.30	0.30	0.54	0.58	0.31	0.33	0.34	0.36
MnO	0.16	0.16	0.19	0.20	0.16	0.17	0.16	0.16
CO_2	--	.02	--	.01	--	.01	--	.03
Cl	--	--	--	.022	--	--	--	.018
F	--	.029	--	.061	--	.030	--	.037
Cr_2O_3	--	.05	--	--	--	<0.02	--	<0.02
Type of sample			segregation vein	segregation vein				
Contains glass?	yes	yes	yes	yes	yes	yes	yes	yes
Temperature before quench	high	high	high	high	high	high	high	high

41

Table A4d. X-ray fluorescence analyses of core from drill hole KI75-1 compared with gravimetric analyses, all in weight percent. Sample annotations as in Helz and others (1994).

	1	2	3	4
Field no.	KI75-1-50.8	KI75-1-50.8	KI75-1-125	KI75-1-125
Lab. no.	D-103843	D-103843	W-214316	W-214316
Job no.		PE74		BD25
Analysis type	XRF	gravimetric	XRF	gravimetric
SiO_2	49.68	49.52	50.41	50.62
Al_2O_3	12.69	12.91	12.31	12.51
Fe_2O_3 (total)	12.35	12.28	13.71	13.61
FeO	--		--	
MgO	8.94	9.07	5.96	5.94
CaO	10.44	10.54	9.46	9.52
Na_2O	2.30	2.33	2.70	2.78
K_2O	0.65	0.62	0.93	0.94
H_2O+	--	.17	--	.10
H_2O-	--	.02	--	.05
TiO_2	3.09	3.11	4.26	4.21
P_2O_5	0.32	0.30	0.47	0.45
MnO	0.17	0.17	0.18	0.18
CO_2	--	.03	--	.01
Cl	--	.008	--	.017
F	--	.031	--	.062
Cr_2O_3	--	.06	--	<0.01
Type of sample			segregation vein	segregation vein
Contains glass?	no	no	yes?	yes?
Temperature before quench	low	low	medium	medium

Table A4e. X-ray fluorescence analyses of core from drill hole KI79-1 compared with gravimetric analyses, all in weight percent. "XRF recheck" indicates sample re-analyzed for cause, as discussed in text. Sample annotations as in Helz and others (1994).

	1	2	3	4	5	6	7	8
Field no.	KI79-1-141.0	KI79-1-141.0	KI79-1-150.3	KI79-1-150.3	KI79-1-160	KI79-1-170	KI79-1-175.0	KI79-1-175.0
Lab. no.	W-223014	W-223014	W-223013	W-223013	W-256772	W-256773	W-223010	W-223010
Job no.		BK52		BK52	CJ13	CJ13		BK52
Analysis type	XRF	gravimetric	XRF	gravimetric	XRF recheck	XRF recheck	XRF	gravimetric
SiO2	49.24	49.60	47.92	47.74	48.4	47.7	47.29	47.07
Al2O3	12.44	12.84	10.94	11.30	11.6	10.9	10.22	10.27
Fe2O3 (total)	12.00	11.69	12.70	12.41	11.9	12.2	12.97	12.66
FeO								
MgO	10.45	10.42	14.86	14.75	13.7	15.0	17.16	17.08
CaO	10.57	10.70	9.79	9.84	10.5	10.1	9.32	9.47
Na2O	2.15	2.19	1.77	1.88	1.79	1.64	1.60	1.63
K2O	0.56	0.57	0.43	0.46	0.45	0.41	0.40	0.41
H2O+	--	.06	--	.05	--	--	--	.11
H2O-	--	.02	--	.02	--	--	--	.01
TiO2	2.76	2.77	2.20	2.23	2.20	2.01	1.92	1.96
P2O5	0.28	0.26	0.23	0.19	0.24	0.22	0.21	0.18
MnO	0.16	0.16	0.17	0.17	0.16	0.17	0.17	0.17
CO2	--	.02	--	.01	--	--	--	.012
Cl	--	.017	--	.020	--	--	--	.039
F	--	.03	--	.030	--	--	--	.030
Cr2O3	--	.10	--	.14	--	--	--	0.18
Type of sample					equivalent to KI79-1-159.5	equivalent to KI79-1-170.2		
Contains glass?	no	no	no	no	yes	yes	yes	yes
Temperature before quench	medium	medium	medium	medium	high	high	high	high

43

Table A4e. X-ray fluorescence and gravimetric analyses of core from drill hole KI79-1 (continued).

Field no.	9 KI79-1-189.0	10 KI79-1-189.0	11 KI79-1-203.7	12 KI79-1-203.7
Lab. no.	W-210876	W-210876	W-210878	W-210878
Job no.		BA56		BA56
Analysis type	XRF	gravimetric	XRF	gravimetric
SiO2	46.04	45.85	45.64	45.55
Al2O3	8.94	8.93	8.33	8.19
Fe2O3 (total)	13.94	13.75	13.53	13.37
FeO	--		--	
MgO	20.84	20.72	22.98	22.68
CaO	7.99	8.05	8.10	8.17
Na2O	1.36	1.36	1.16	1.17
K2O	0.32	0.32	0.26	0.25
H2O+	--	.06	--	.04
H2O-	--	.01	--	.00
TiO2	1.61	1.52	1.30	1.27
P2O5	0.17	0.16	0.15	0.12
MnO	0.18	0.18	0.18	0.17
CO2	--	.01	--	.01
Cl	--	.008	--	.012
F	--	.022	--	.018
Cr2O3	--	0.16	--	0.22
Type of sample			deepest core	deepest core
Contains glass?	yes	yes	yes	yes
Temperature before quench	high	high	high	high

44

Table A4f. X-ray fluorescence analyses of core from drill hole KI79-3 compared with gravimetric analyses, all in weight percent. Sample annotations as in Helz and others (1994).

	1	2	3	4	5	6	7	8
Field no.	KI79-3-145.1	KI79-3-145.1	KI79-3-150.3	KI79-3-150.3	KI79-3-160.3	KI79-3-160.3	KI79-3-166.1	KI79-3-166.1
Lab. no.	W-210495	W-210495	W-210496	W-210496	W-210497	W-210497	W-210498	W-210498
Job no.		BA23		BA23		BA23		BA23
Analysis type	XRF	gravimetric	XRF	gravimetric	XRF	gravimetric	XRF	gravimetric
SiO_2	44.08	43.94	48.40	48.44	47.46	47.37	43.56	43.40
Al_2O_3	6.54	6.59	11.52	11.72	10.72	10.82	5.76	5.88
Fe_2O_3 (total)	15.89	15.70	11.87	11.72	12.81	12.68	16.74	16.55
FeO	--	--	--	--	--	--	--	--
MgO	26.35	26.16	13.58	13.51	16.11	16.05	27.73	27.41
CaO	5.81	5.84	10.70	10.77	9.28	9.35	5.15	5.21
Na_2O	1.03	1.08	1.78	1.82	1.72	1.74	0.94	0.97
K_2O	0.23	0.23	0.43	0.44	0.43	0.43	0.24	0.24
H_2O+	--	.04	--	.04	--	.07	--	.05
H_2O-	--	.00	--	.01	--	.02	--	.01
TiO_2	1.38	1.34	2.14	2.07	2.14	2.07	1.29	1.24
P_2O_5	0.12	0.10	0.22	0.19	0.21	0.18	0.14	0.10
MnO	0.20	0.20	0.16	0.16	0.17	0.17	0.21	0.20
CO_2	--	.01	--	.01	--	.01	--	.01
Cl	--	.005	--	.007	--	.012	--	.007
F	--	.014	--	.026	--	.027	--	.016
Cr_2O_3	--	0.18	--	0.14	--	0.13	--	0.20
Type of sample	vorb	vorb					vorb	vorb
Contains glass?	trace	trace	no	no	yes	yes	yes	yes
Temperature before quench	medium	medium	medium	medium	high	high	high	high

45

Table A4f. X-ray fluorescence and gravimetric analyses of core from drill hole KI79-3 (continued).

Field no.	9 KI79-3-169.1	10 KI79-3-169.1	11 KI79-3-172.8	12 KI79-3-172.8	13 KI79-3-172.8
Lab. no.	W-210499	W-210499	W-210500	W-210500	W-256774
Job no.		BA23		BA23	CJ13
Analysis type	XRF	gravimetric	XRF	gravimetric	new XRF
SiO2	46.88	46.67	46.79	46.58	47.0
Al2O3	9.84	10.07	9.66	9.86	9.73
Fe2O3 (total)	13.03	12.83	12.99	12.85	13.0
FeO	--		--		(10.1)
MgO	18.37	18.21	18.80	18.71	18.8
CaO	8.96	9.04	8.87	8.97	8.92
Na2O	1.50	1.52	1.48	1.49	1.41
K2O	0.36	0.35	0.35	0.35	0.37
H2O+	--	.05	--	.05	<0.01
H2O-	--	.01	--	.01	.21
TiO2	1.80	1.73	1.77	1.70	1.77
P2O5	0.19	0.16	0.19	0.16	0.20
MnO	0.18	0.17	0.18	0.17	0.18
CO2	--	.01	--	.01	.01
Cl	--	.010	--	.010	.018
F	--	.022	--	.022	.30
Cr2O3	--	0.16	--	0.17	0.18
Type of sample					coarse split
Contains glass?	yes	yes	yes	yes	yes
Temperature before quench	high	high	high	high	high

46

Table A4g. X-ray fluorescence analyses of core from drill holes KI81-1 and KI81-2 compared with gravimetric analyses, all in weight percent. Sample annotations as in Helz and others (1994).

	1	2	3	4
Field no.	KI81-1-250.0	KI81-1-250.0	KI81-2-88.6	KI81-2-88.6
Lab. no.	W-214110	W-214110	W-232725	W-232725
Job no.		BD02		BR98
Analysis type	XRF	gravimetric	XRF	gravimetric
SiO_2	44.81	44.66	56.60	57.07
Al_2O_3	7.43	7.40	12.41	12.86
Fe_2O_3 (total)	14.12	13.91	13.15	12.90
FeO	--	--	--	
MgO	25.63	25.43	2.45	2.37
CaO	7.06	7.14	5.90	6.08
Na_2O	1.00	1.02	3.62	3.55
K_2O	0.22	0.21	1.98	1.90
H_2O+	--	.03	--	.11
H_2O-	--	.02	--	.07
TiO_2	1.12	1.05	2.60	2.59
P_2O_5	0.12	0.10	1.01	0.96
MnO	0.18	0.18	0.18	0.18
CO_2	--	.01	--	<.01
Cl	--	.008	--	.028
F	--	.016	--	.11
Cr_2O_3	--	0.24	--	<0.01
Type of sample			vein-in-vein	vein-in-vein
Contains glass?	yes	yes	no	no
Temperature before quench	high	high	low	low

47